Innovation Diffusion and New Product Growth

RELEVANT KNOWLEDGE SERIES

Innovation Diffusion and New Product Growth

EITAN MULLER
RENANA PERES
VIJAY MAHAJAN

MARKETING SCIENCE INSTITUTE
Cambridge, Massachusetts

Contents

Foreword

Innovation provides new ways to create value for customers, yielding growth and profitability for firms. For this reason, it has been a top MSI research priority for many years, reflecting widespread interest among our member companies. The topic of this book, the ninth in our Relevant Knowledge Series, is diffusion of innovations: the process by which new products and services penetrate markets driven by social influences. Some readers may recall the path-breaking work on this topic by Dr. Frank Bass—now almost 50 years ago. His model is the foundation for the rich array of models of innovation diffusion that exist today.

These new models tackle the important issues facing firms introducing innovations into the marketplace: rapid proliferation of information, social networks, intense competition, enhanced branding, the growth of service markets, attractive opportunities in the developing world, and globalization. In addition, they apply to many of our most exciting and dynamic markets: high technology products, telecommunications, entertainment, health and pharmaceuticals, durable goods, and products with long inter-purchase times.

Models of innovation diffusion now reflect the reality of connected customers. A major contribution of this book is that it explains how social influences among customers operate, with or without their explicit knowledge, including all the interdependencies among consumers that affect various market players. The authors, Eitan Muller, Renana Peres, and Vijay Mahajan, provide a valuable service to marketing practitioners and academics by tracing these mechanisms and revealing new insights for managers.

One important insight for managers is that innovation diffusion is highly dependent on diverse social interactions of consumers, as well as word-of-mouth communications. Research has shown that signals of the product's functionality (e.g., its quality and risk) and its social consequences influence adoption. For example, the adoption of the innovation by people in the "right" group can signal members of this group to adopt it—without any interpersonal ties or interpersonal communication!

This book is essential reading for any practitioner or academic who is interested in how innovation grows sales over time. We are pleased to add it to MSI's Relevant Knowledge Series. We thank the authors for sharing their expertise and creating this insightful contribution to our series.

Ruth N. Bolton
MSI Executive Director 2009–11

Executive Summary

For firms launching innovative products and services in today's complex and erratic markets, the ability to model and predict the penetration of these innovations into the markets is critical. Diffusion research is the field in marketing which seeks to understand the spread of an innovation by modeling the entire new product life cycle—from launch till the end of the product's life.

Five decades of research has contributed greatly to our understanding of the evolution of innovation markets. Research is constantly moving beyond the basic diffusion scenario, developed by Frank Bass in 1969, of a monopoly of durable goods, toward exploring a variety of scenarios and customer interactions.

We can describe with greater accuracy turning points in the product life cycle, including takeoffs, saddles, and technological substitution. We have a better knowledge of the effect of competition, advertising, and pricing on growth, and we can describe how growth of products is influenced by their diffusion in other countries. We have begun exploring how the structure of the social network influences the contagion process. The focus given to specific industries, such as entertainment, telecommunication, services, and pharmaceuticals, has revealed their idiosyncrasies and provided managers with better tools to manage their diffusion processes.

While research in diffusion is wide-ranging, a number of general findings have emerged. These are summarized below and discussed at length in the chapters that follow.

The Mechanisms That Generate Diffusion

New product or service adoption occurs as a result of the combination of two types of influences—*external influences,* which are the marketing activities of the firms, such as advertising, sampling, and sales force, and *internal influences,* which relate to influences among customers. These influences take three forms: First are direct consumer communications such as word-of-mouth. Second are signals, which are the inferences derived with no direct communication (*functional*, denoting product quality or credibility, and *social*, signaling the social desirability or prestige of owning a product). Third are network externalities, which describe the increased utility some products have with the increase of the installed base. For example, the utility of a customer from a fax machine or from email services depends on the number of other individuals who have already adopted the product.

We therefore define diffusion of innovations as follows:
Innovation diffusion is the process of the market penetration of new products and services driven by social influences. Such influences include all the interdependencies among consumers that affect various market players, with and without their explicit knowledge.

Because diffusion depends so heavily on these social influences, even highly successful products tend to grow very slowly. Higher network effects, for example, can substantially attenuate growth in early stages, as consumers "wait" for a critical mass of adopters to increase product utility. A typical result indicates that, it took, on average, more than six years for innovations to reach 25% of their market potential, slightly over nine years to reach 50%, and about 18 years to reach 95% of their respective market potential.

Turning Points in the Product Life Cycle

The life cycle of an innovation encompasses three turning points: *takeoff, peak of growth*, and *technological substitution* of the innovation by a new and improved version. For some products, a *saddle*, i.e., a slump in sales after the initial growth, is observed. Takeoff occurs early in the lifecycle and is the start of rapid growth. At takeoff, external factors such as price, product type, and cultural heterogeneity interact with consumer interactions and interdependencies to generate a rapid increase in sales. On average, takeoff occurs six years after product launch when the penetration rate is 1.7% of market potential.

A saddle describes a sudden decrease in sales during the early growth stage, after the takeoff, that is followed by another rapid increase in sales that eventually develops into full adoption. A saddle can be explained by a gap in communication between two groups of adopters—the early adopters and the main market. Stockpiling, changes in technology, industry performance, or macroeconomic events can also contribute to the formation of a saddle.

Saddle was observed in one-third to one-half of consumer electronic products, with a relative depth of 25% and on average duration of four years. Saddle is also frequent in technological business markets.

The diffusion process continues to the peak of sales, and ends with the adoption of the product by the entire market potential, or when the innovation is substituted with more advanced products and technology generations. The entry of a new technology generation complicates growth dynamics. It is usually considered to increase the market potential, however, this enlarged pool of customers may cannibalize the new technology's potential by adopting the older generation or by skipping a generation altogether.

Spatial Effects

Many new products and services penetrate simultaneously in more than one market or country. Diffusion processes in different countries are influenced by each other through word-of-mouth communications, signals, and network externalities. One of the major findings of the studies on cross-country influences is that entry time lag has a positive influence on the diffusion process, that is, countries that introduce a given innovation later show a faster diffusion process and a faster time-to-takeoff than the initial adopting countries.

Looking for the sources of difference in diffusion speed between countries, studies investigated economic, cultural, and market structure sources. Generally, diffusion is faster in countries with high levels of wealth, income inequality, homogenous population, less uncertainly avoidance, collectivism, masculinity, and power distance. Diffusion of brown goods is faster than that of white goods. Regulation has a positive influence on diffusion, and the effect of competition is mixed.

Diffusion and Competition

While innovative categories may start as monopolies, many quickly develop to include multiple competing brands. Competition complicates the diffusion market, since the diffusion of each brand is influenced by the diffusion of competing brands. The process of brand adoption is not yet clear—we do not know if consumers first decide to adopt the category and then choose brand, or whether the adoption is done at the brand level. It is also not clear whether a new brand in the market increases the market potential, and how to measure the level of market potential of each brand.

An interesting recent finding is that consumer interactions go within brand and across brands. Thus, firms enjoy the within-brand influence of their customers, but also the cross-brand influence on potential adopters from the customers of the competitors.

Effects of Pricing and Advertising

Firms influence the diffusion process through the marketing mix elements: price, marketing communications, product, and distribution channels, where the first two received most research attention.

An interesting finding is that due to the critical role of internal influences, firms can make good forecasts of the diffusion process even when they do not have data on past and future advertising expenses and price.

The internal dynamics influences optimal pricing decisions; thus, studies show that it might be worthwhile for firms to subsidize early adopters, and reduce the price of the first technology generation in order to increase future demand. Surprisingly, in some cases, competition enables firms to charge a higher price for the first generation.

Diffusion and Social Networks

The last decade has seen a number of attempts to bridge individual decision-making and aggregate category demand by exploring social network processes. Individual-level models of these processes have incorporated heterogeneity into the diffusion framework, and separated the effects of word-of-mouth, signals, and network externalities. Some empirical studies have explored the influence of the social network structure on growth. Much of the research attention has been on the role of central individuals (influentials, social hubs) on the overall growth process.

A methodology that is being increasingly used to model diffusion on social networks is agent-based modeling, which simulates the market as an ensemble of interconnected units, representing consumers. Using these methods researchers showed how individual decisions aggregate to create the diffusion curve we see in real markets. They explored the influence of weak and strong ties, demonstrated the formation of saddles, explored questions as to the seeding of the new product in the social network, and elaborated our ability to forecast the success or failure of a new product.

New Product Growth in Specific Industries

Much research was dedicated toward exploring the diffusion patterns in specific industries, especially entertainment, services, telecommunications, and pharmaceuticals. Each of these industries illuminates a different aspect of diffusion—entertainment products are influenced by a strong pre-launch accumulated demand, services bring the issue of customer churn to diffusion, telecommunications emphasize network externalities, and pharmaceuticals—the effect of intermediaries, and marketing communication methods such as sampling and detailing.

Choosing the Right Model

Managers who wish to implement the body of knowledge and use diffusion modeling for planning, diagnostics, and forecasting often face the dilemma of which model or method will best describe the complex environment in which they operate. Choosing the right model and the method for parameter estimations depends on the nature of the innovation, the market, the managerial task, and the quality and amount of available data.

Introduction

At the end of 2008, 4 billion people around the world were using mobile phones. Launched in 1981 in Scandinavia, mobile phone service has become a part of everyday life for over half of the world's population in 211 countries. The massive penetration of mobile telephony is not exceptional: Many commonly used products and services such as DVDs, personal computers, digital cameras, online banking, and the Internet were not known to consumers three decades ago, and firms invest continually in future product and service innovations.

There is substantial research on modeling the diffusion of innovations, much of it based on the well-known Bass model developed in 1969, which assumes a single-market monopoly of durable goods in a homogenous, fully connected social system. That scenario no longer describes the diffusion process in today's markets. Reflecting current market trends, diffusion modeling has been extended to incorporate issues such as the rapid proliferation of information, globalization, competition, partially connected social networks, and growth of service markets.

In this monograph, we review the diffusion literature: We first review the classic diffusion scenarios, then focus on more recent research from the last two decades and offer a unified framework for understanding how diffusion occurs in complex markets today. We focus on the diffusion literature in marketing, and do not survey operations research, technological forecasting, behavioral diffusion theory, and economics growth literature.

For academic researchers, our review offers a foundational study of the diffusion literature with an emphasis on shifts in focus and questions that still need to be explored. For marketing managers, understanding the diffusion process is a critical first step to choosing the appropriate modeling tools that reflect the complexities and interdependencies of their particular market scenario. Specifically, we discuss the following managerially relevant issues:

■ Innovation diffusion highly depends not only on word-of-mouth communications but on other social interactions of consumers—including network externalities, functional and social signals—that affect various market players, with and without their explicit knowledge.

■ When observing growth of new products, one is struck by the unbearable slowness of its growth. We explain why growth is slow even for highly successful products.

■ The fact that one needs quite a few data points to estimate the Bass model implies that for pre-launch predictions (when few, if any, data points exist), managers cannot turn to the Bass model for help. We show that one can utilize data on similar products and previous generations of the same base technology, compute the growth pattern parameters, and apply them to the new product.

■ Turning points in the product life cycle such as takeoffs and saddles can be predicted and managed.

■ Diffusion in one country influences diffusion in other countries. A firm can use this to optimize the speed and investment in global launches, as well as to forecast the diffusion of the same product in different countries.

■ The diffusion framework that was traditionally applied to the category level can be used successfully to manage and speed up the introduction of a brand within a competitive product category.

■ In growing markets, pricing decisions and decisions regarding investments in advertising are different than those of mature markets. The diffusion framework provides tools to optimize profits through control of advertising costs and pricing revenues.

■ Social networks can be integrated into the framework of innovation diffusion and are especially useful in cases where the potential adopters' population is clustered, heterogeneous, and displays complex decision processes.

■ Entertainment, telecommunications, services, and pharmaceutical products have their own idiosyncrasies, which influence their diffusion processes. Considering pre-launch demand in entertainment products, network externalities in communication products, customer attrition in services, and intermediaries in pharmaceuticals is essential in order to properly manage their diffusion. Recent diffusion research in these industries provides the tools to do so.

In the chapters that follow, we offer some basics of innovation diffusion and explore the mechanisms that underlie new product growth. We then investigate the Bass diffusion model and its extensions, discuss turning points in the product life cycle, and the spatial dimensions of diffusion. We also address the competitive aspects of new product introduction, in particular highlighting the difference between category and brand growth, as well as the effects of price and advertising, and the role of analysis of individual-level decision making within the social network.

Several models have been developed to describe new product growth in specific industries such as entertainment, telecommunications, services, and pharmaceuticals, and we describe those here. We also offer a flow chart to assist managers in determining which model best suits their industry and market environment. We conclude by identifying questions in need of further research.

It is our hope that this monograph will provide both researchers and managers with a deeper appreciation and understanding of the intricacies involved in assessing, predicting, and managing new product growth in today's multifaceted and erratic market environment.

Acknowledgments

We greatly benefitted from comments and suggestions on previous drafts by Bart Bronnenberg, Deepa Chandrasekaran, Jacob Goldenberg, Towhidul Islam, Trichy Krishnan, Barak Libai, Philip Parker, Ashutod Prasad, Arvind Rangaswamy, John Roberts, Gerard Tellis, Chistophe Van den Bulte, and Charles Weinberg.

Eitan Muller
Renana Peres
Vijay Mahajan

Innovation Diffusion and New Product Growth

1

Understanding Innovation Diffusion

The spread of an innovation in a market is termed *diffusion*. Diffusion research seeks to understand the spread of innovations by modeling their entire new product life cycle from the perspective of communications and consumer interactions.

Traditionally, diffusion models have been based on the model developed by Frank Bass in 1969. The Bass model and its extensions, which will be discussed in depth in Chapter 3, consider the case of a monopoly of a durable good, and investigates the aggregate first-purchase growth of the category in a single market. The social network is assumed to be fully connected and homogenous. An individual in this network adopts the innovation as a result of two types of influences: external influences, that is, advertising and other communications by the firm; and internal influences, resulting from interaction between adopters and potential adopters in the social system, based on word-of-mouth and interpersonal communications (Peres, Muller, and Mahajan 2010; Mahajan, Muller, and Wind 2000; Mahajan, Muller, and Bass 1990; Parker 1994).

The scenario envisioned by the Bass model is no longer adequate to fully describe the diffusion process in many of today's markets. With a growing number of new information, entertainment, and communication products and services, as well as the development of market trends such as globalization and increased competition, diffusion processes have become much more complex than before, challenging the validity of many of the basic assumptions of the Bass model. The diffusion modeling literature since 1990 has attempted to extend the Bass framework for reflecting the increasing complexity of new product growth. Table 1 provides an overview of the main changes in research focus.

Consider the shift from word-of-mouth to social influences as drivers of diffusion. In the past, most of the internal dynamics of diffusion was due to word-of-mouth and communication mechanisms; however, the higher information and media availability these days enables individuals to be influenced by others even without direct communications. Many recent communication innova-

Table 1
Past versus Current Research Focus of Diffusion Modeling

Diffusion Modeling 1960–1990	Diffusion Modeling since 1990
Word-of-mouth as driver	Consumer interdependencies as drivers
Monotonically increasing penetration curve	Turning points and irregularities in the penetration curve
Temporal	Temporal and spatial
Industry-level analysis	Brand-level analysis
Aggregate or segment-based models	Individual-level models
Fully connected networks	Partially connected and small-world networks
Products	Services
Forecasting	Managerial diagnostics

tions, such as the Internet or mobile phones, are network goods, that is, their utility for the individual depends on the number of other individuals who have already adopted the product. This influence of the installed base occurs without direct communication from other users. Thus, research moved beyond word-of-mouth or direct customer interactions to investigate the social influences that drive growth.

Similarly, as the gap between the technology-oriented early adopters and the main market widens, and as products are more rapidly replaced by newer technological generations, the smooth and monotonically increasing penetration curve is called into question. Due to market trends such as globalization and increased competition, many products penetrate simultaneously in more than one country, as in the case of mobile phones, which were launched throughout Scandinavia within a single year. Researchers must now ask how diffusion in a given country is influenced by interaction with individuals in other countries. Regarding competition, modeling the category level or regarding the innovation as a monopoly are not sufficient. Products today enjoy shorter monopoly periods, and a typical product category consists of a portfolio of brands that penetrate simultaneously to the market. Recent studies explore how interactions between brands in a portfolio influence the growth of each brand and of the entire category.

Choice processes have also become more complicated as innovations increasingly involve the choice of both product and service providers. Further, the definition of category is sometimes ambiguous (is an iPhone a mobile handset, a music player, or a PDA?). Thus, research has started to track individual-level decision processes as their influence on aggregate behavior becomes more acute. Services occupy a growing volume of commercial activity, and categories such as entertainment and pharmaceuticals are becoming more significant. The penetration patterns for these industries, involving churn, rapid diffusion cycles, and distribution structure, differ greatly from traditional durable goods. Recent diffusion research invests increasing efforts in these industries. Previous research was generally aimed at forecasting; current research places more emphasis on managerial diagnostics.

This change of focus is ongoing. Future developments such as the rapid evolution of online social communities, emergence of innovation markets in developing countries, enhanced branding, and the use of sophisticated distribution mechanisms will require further changes and modifications of concepts and models. Diffusion research, loyal to its mission to provide a comprehensive description of life cycle processes, is continuously striving to fill the knowledge gaps in order to assist managers and firms with the enormous challenges of successful introduction of new products and services into tomorrow's markets.

2
Beyond a Theory of Communications

A fundamental question in understanding diffusion of innovations concerns the market mechanisms that generate and enhance the penetration of an innovation into a market. Mainstream diffusion modeling regards the diffusion of an innovation as a social contagion process, namely, a process driven by the interactions among members of a social system. Early diffusion modeling did not explore the nature of each type of social interaction, and assumes that they mainly consist of interpersonal communications and imitation. In this chapter we suggest a broader view of the social influences that drive diffusion, and discuss an alternative approach which views customer heterogeneity as the main driving force of diffusion.

Types of Social Influence

During the last two decades, research has begun to disentangle the different types of social interactions by modeling them and exploring their influence on aggregate growth. Behavioral and modeling literature look for motivations and mechanisms for social interactions, the different ways they influence individual adoption, and how individual decisions create aggregate growth patterns.

This body of recent findings suggests that diffusion theory should be extended from its traditional scope as a theory of interpersonal communications to encompass social influences of all kinds.

We therefore define diffusion of innovations as follows:
Innovation diffusion is the process of the market penetration of new products and services driven by social influences. Such influences include all the interdependencies among consumers that affect various market players, with and without their explicit knowledge.

Under this definition, new product and service adoption is generated by a wide spectrum of influences which can be classified into three forms: word-of-mouth communications, signals (functional and social), and network externalities.

Word-of-Mouth Communications In word-of-mouth communications, consumers actively engage in collecting and processing information from previous adopters through verbal or written communication such as conversations, email, or participation in user groups and social activities. The less frequent the purchase, the higher the perceived risk, the higher the monetary value, and the more involved the consumer is with the product, the more likely the consumer is to engage in word-of-mouth (Rosen 2000).

There is debate as to how a firm should enhance word-of-mouth transmission for its innovative products: while some approaches encourage focusing on "influentials" (Iyengar, Van den Bulte, and Valente 2008; Weimann 1994), others claim that approaching the most easily influenced population is more effective (Watts and Dodds 2007). While industry practice regards the word-of-mouth distributed by loyal customers as a major driver of firms' long-term profitability (Reichheld 2003), others argue that the word-of-mouth of less loyal customers is more effective (Godes and Mayzlin 2009).

Signals Signals can be defined as any market information other than personal recommendation that can be used by a potential adopter to make an adoption decision. The "imitation" mentioned in the early diffusion literature is an example of a signal. Signals can convey functional information as well as social information as to the status and group identity associated with adopting the product.

Functional signals contain information regarding the acceptance of the product in the social system, its quality, and the amount of risk it involves. For example, in many cases, the number of other individuals that perform a certain action can be used as a signal to a given individual regarding the norms of the group (Granovetter 1978). This may be the case for new product adoption, where the number of previous adopters signals better product quality, especially when there is widespread uncertainty surrounding the product. Similarly, in international penetration of new products, consumers in one country have a positive adoption effect on the consumers in other countries. Consumers in the other countries do not actually have to engage in conversations. A French consumer can be influenced by the fact that the product is successful in Japan even without talking to any Japanese consumer—what he observes is a signal. The existence of competition and the entry of major players into the market can serve as signals of the credibility of a new product.

Social signals contain information on the social consequences of adopting the product. Through their purchases, individuals seek to either maintain social differences or to signal group identity (Bourdieu 1984). These signals are transmitted to other individuals who follow the consumption behavior of people in their aspiration group (Simmel 1957; Van den Bulte and Wuyts 2007; Van den Bulte and Joshi 2007). Social signals operate vertically and horizontally. Vertically, they indicate the status of the adopter. Recent research indicates that competition for status is an important growth driver, sometimes more important than interpersonal ties (Burt 1987), and that the speed of diffusion increases in societies that are more sensitive to status differences (Van den Bulte and Stremersch 2004). Social signals are also transmitted horizontally, to indicate group identity. Thus, the adoption of an innovation by people in the "right" group signals members in this group to adopt it (Berger and Heath 2007), and members of other groups to avoid adoption (Berger and Heath 2008).

Note that signals can be transmitted by a variety of means, such as the traditional media, the Web, observations, or even interpersonal communications. However, signals can be distinguished from word-of-mouth in that signals convey information about the product and market status *other than personal recommendations*. From the modeling point of view, word-of-mouth and signals are quite different: Signals do not require interpersonal ties, while word-of-mouth is dependent on interpersonal ties between adopters and potential adopters.

Adoption due to signals is sometimes termed *informational cascade* (Golder and Tellis 2004, 1997), defined as the tendency of individuals to adopt a behavior based on the value of the signal they derive from the behavior of previous adopters (Golder and Tellis 2004). Although informational cascade can be created by interpersonal communications, the term is usually used to describe influence achieved through imitation of other individuals, opinion leaders, or social hubs that use the product.

Network Externalities Network goods are products or services that generate network externalities, i.e., the utility of the product to a consumer increases as more consumers adopt the new product (Rohlfs 2001). Network externalities can be direct, where the utility is directly affected by the number of other users, such as in the case of telecommunications services, or indirect, where utility increases with the number of users of another, complementary product, such as in the case of DVD players and content (Stremersch et al. 2007; Binken and Stremersch 2009). Network externalities do not require interpersonal communications: Potential adopters can determine penetration level from the media, or simply by observing retail offerings. For example, during the transition from videotapes to DVDs, a consumer had merely to walk into Blockbuster and observe the amount of aisle space devoted to VHS versus DVD in order to understand that DVDs were about to become the new standard.

Another distinction between types of externalities is whether their impact on diffusion is local or global. Under global externalities, a consumer takes into account an entire social system when considering the impact of the number of adopters on utility, whereas under local externalities, a consumer considers adoption in relation to his or her close social network. Research is gradually moving from considering only global externalities toward exploring local externalities (Binken and Stremersch 2009; Tucker 2008). The marketing decisions of the firm can influence the type of externalities: competing standards growth will probably invoke a global effect, since the "verdict" on what eventually becomes the winning standard depends on the total number of users. In contrast, the family program of a mobile provider might evoke a local effect since it involves only the local social system.

Intuitively, network externalities are considered to have a positive influence on a product's sales and penetration (Nair, Chintagunta, and Dubé 2004; Tellis, Yin, and Niraj 2009). However, some recent studies show a *negative* effect of network externalities, either on early-stage growth (Goldenberg, Libai, and Muller 2010), or on the survival of pioneers (Srinivasan, Lilien, and Rangaswamy 2004). This duality exists since in network goods, adopters delay their adoption until a large enough number of other people has adopted the product (e.g., what is the utility of a fax machine if only a single consumer adopted it?). In early diffusion stages the need to reach a critical mass for adoption delays the diffusion. Later on, this critical mass is reached for most consumers, and the positive effect on penetration is dominant.

As mentioned above, the classical diffusion modeling interprets the effects of previous cumulative adopters on current sales in terms of personal communications (Mahajan, Muller, and Bass 1990). However, the social contagion process they describe can be also explained by signals and network externalities. Disentangling the contagion process into the various forms of interactions is of managerial importance. If, for example, adopting the new product sends a strong social signal, the firm might want to emphasize its adoption by leading individuals. However, for a network good, a better investment of resources would be to increase the product's compatibility to existing standards in order to avoid the chilling effect of network externalities. New models, which represent explicitly these three forms of interactions, will help firms to better monitor and control the influence processes within their target market in order to enhance the diffusion.

Social Influence versus Consumer Heterogeneity

A new research branch has emerged as an alternative to consumer-interaction–based diffusion. This viewpoint argues that the major driver of growth of new products is consumer *heterogeneity*, rather than consumer interaction. The heterogeneity approach claims that the population is heterogeneous in innovativeness, price sensitivity, and needs, leading to heterogeneity in propensity to adopt. Thus, innovators are the least patient in adopting, whereas laggards are the most patient. Often patience is inversely related to affordability, willingness to pay, or reservation price (Song and Chintagunta 2003; Golder and Tellis 1998). The dynamics of market volume are determined by the shape of the distribution of the "patience" as it faces falling prices. If incomes are log-normally distributed in the population, then growth is S-shaped (Golder and Tellis 1997). This line of research implies that the current diffusion-based research has overemphasized the influence of word-of-mouth communication (see Van den Bulte and Stremersch 2004; Van den Bulte and Lilien 2001).

Figure 1 illustrates the range of possible drivers of new product diffusion, arranged by the level of direct interpersonal communications they involve.

Figure 1
Market Factors That Drive the Diffusion of Innovations

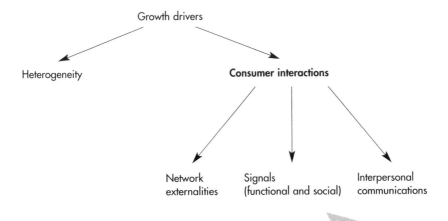

Level of direct interpersonal communication involved

3
The Bass Model

The best-known model in diffusion research is the Bass model (Bass 1969). Since publication of the model in *Management Science*, it has been cited over 600 times, and it forms the basis for nearly all the models in this book.

Model Description

Assume a market with potential m. At each point in time, new adopters join the market as a result of influences of two kinds: external and internal. *External influences* are the marketing activities of firms in the market, such as advertising. The probability of adopting at a certain point in time as a result of an external influence is denoted by p. *Internal influences* are market dependencies and interactions. The probability of adopting at a certain point in time as an outcome of an internal influence from a single adopter is denoted by q. Traditionally, q represented word-of-mouth communications. However, the more recent interpretation we present in this monograph regards the parameter q as representing *social influences* in all their manifestations: word-of-mouth communications, signals, and network externalities.

The Bass model was inspired by earlier models for evolution of epidemics, such as the SIR model: Susceptible, Infected, Removed, illustrated in Figure 2. Consider the case of an epidemic, such as cholera, in a given community. Since there is no known natural immunization, the entire population is found in the top box of Figure 2—the Susceptibles. There are two ways to get infected: by an external source, usually contaminated water, or by an internal source, that is, physical contact with a sick person. Once a person is infected, there are two ways to leave this group: to die or to recover. Under the first circumstance, the person is removed from the epidemic process and under the latter, the person is susceptible again, as if he or she never got the disease in the first place. (More information on the SIR model and its variants can be found at Bailey 1957; Giraldo and Palacio 2008; and van den Broek and Heesterbeek 2007.)

Figure 2
The SIR Epidemiology Model

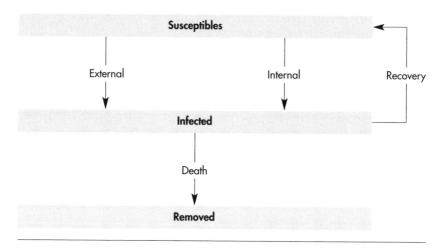

Figure 3
The Bass Model

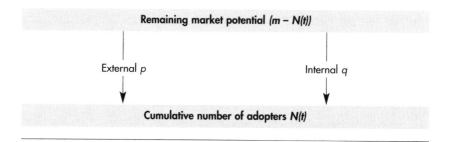

This model can be applied to the diffusion of an innovation as follows (see Figure 3). If $N(t)$ is the cumulative number of adopters at time t, then the remaining market potential is $m - N(t)$. A given fraction of this untapped potential adopts in the next period, that is, $p \cdot (m - N(t))$. The internal flow is a bit more intricate: If the current number of adopters is $N(t)$ (read: the number of infected people), then their overall influence is $q \cdot N(t)$. At each point in time they are exposed to the fraction of $(m - N(t))/m$ people who has not yet adopted (read: the healthy individuals) and might infect them with a probability q.

Note that, similar to the epidemiological model, the Bass model focuses only on the influence of adopters on people who had not yet adopted. To illustrate, if two adopters of iPhone meet each other, they might congratulate each other on their wisdom in having adopted iPhone, but no new adopters will come out of this meeting. For the latter to happen we need one "sick" (adopted) and one "healthy" (not yet adopted) individual to meet and exchange the "bacteria" (social influence and information about the iPhone).

Combining the two terms yields the following equation, aptly called the Bass equation:

$$\frac{dN(t)}{dt} = \left(p + \frac{qN(t)}{m} \right) \cdot (m - N(t)) \tag{1a}$$

Denoting by $x(t)$ the adoption percentage at time t, that is, $x(t) = N(t) / m$, the percentage of new adopters at time t can be equivalently described by the following equation:

$$\frac{dx(t)}{dt} = (p + qx(t)) \cdot (1 - x(t)) \tag{1b}$$

If each adopter buys exactly one unit, these equations describe the sales growth of the innovation that follows a bell shape, while the cumulative function is a classical S-shaped function. Figure 4 shows the Bass equation when applied to the diffusion of mobile phones in Norway from 1981 through 2004 ($p = .0046$; $q = .332$; $m = 4.99$ millions). The bell-shaped curve represented in the top panel depicts the number of new subscribers, i.e., sales growth, while the S-shaped curve in the bottom panel depicts the cumulative number of subscribers.

Use and Limitations of the Bass Model

Determining Model Parameters The Bass model parameters p, q, and m can be estimated from adoption data, usually by using non-linear least squares. The average values of q and p for durable goods were found to be $p = .03$ and $q = .38$ (Sultan, Farley, and Lehmann 1990). Values for a variety of durable goods can

Figure 4
The Bass Penetration Function, Using the Parameters for Mobile
Phones in Norway 1982–2004: $p = .0046$, $q = .33$, $m = 4,997,853$

New subscribers

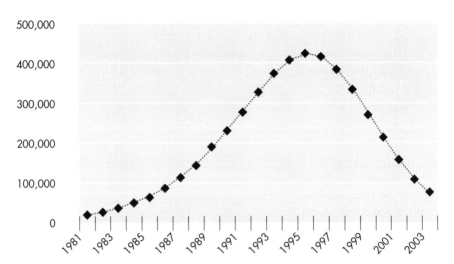

Cumulative subscribers

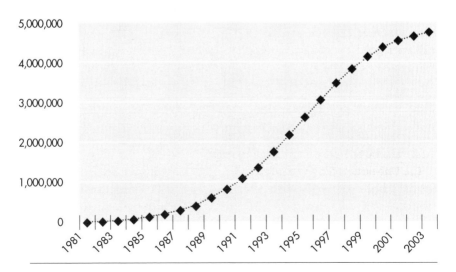

be found in Lilien, Rangaswamy, and Van den Bulte (2000). Estimation issues are also discussed in Jiang, Bass, and Bass (2006), Boswijk and Franses (2005), Van den Bulte and Stremersch (2003), and Van den Bulte and Lilien (1997).

Knowing the model parameters is important for forecasting and diagnosing the further temporal growth of the new product. This task is crucial as it pertains to a number of critical marketing decisions regarding product attributes, pricing and promotion, subsidizing complementary hardware or software, and distribution (Moon 2003; Ofek 2005). In many cases, managers want to do the forecasting prior to launching the innovation. For such pre-launch predictions, managers cannot use the Bass model as the parameter estimates are unstable in the presence of only a few data points (Putsis and Srinivasan 2000). A reliable estimate of the diffusion process parameters requires sales data from introduction through peak of sales (Srinivasan and Mason 1986). To address this issue, marketing scholars have proposed using longitudinal data on previous generations or analogous products, computing the growth pattern parameters (other than the market potential), and using them on the new generation. This, of course, assumes that these parameters do not vary much across technology generations, an assumption that will be discussed in length in the next chapter.

What Categories Lend Themselves to the Bass Model? High-technology products naturally, but not exclusively, lend themselves to the Bass diffusion framework. In general, other products that can be described by the Bass model and its extensions include durable goods or long-term services; search goods, whose attributes can be discovered prior to the actual purchase (as opposed to experience goods, whose attributes can only be assessed post purchase); products with high perceived risk such as discontinuous radical innovations; products with infrequent inter-purchase time (as opposed to FMCGs, fast-moving consumer goods, whose success crucially depends on repeat purchase); and high involvement and high priced products. Because of the commitment an adopter makes when purchasing the products, the potential risk reduction, and the monetary and emotional investment involved, in all of these categories, potential adopters tend to invest in search, such as listening, viewing, or reading advertisements, to actively participate in word-of-mouth activities, and to engage and be open to other social influences.

The Unbearable Slowness of New Product Growth For many innovations, especially high-technology ones, it is quite common for an overzealous entrepreneur to present a venture capitalist, or VP product development, with a well-thought-out calculation of market potential and then declare: "Of this market potential, we'll reach 50% within two years." This fast penetration, unfortunately, does not happen in reality. Though one observes certain acceleration in the speed of diffusion processes over time, as we will discuss in the next chapter, the process is still painfully slow. For example, Mahajan, Muller, and Srivastava (1990) observe the growth of 14 successful durable products in the U.S. and report that on average it took more than six years for these innovations to reach 25% of their market potential, slightly over nine years to reach 50%, and about 18 years to reach 95% of their respective market potential.

The reason is that the social influences, which generate the successful diffusion, are responsible, at the same time, for the negative implications for the speed of the process. From the Bass equation (Equation 1), it is straightforward to see that the flow of adopters that is generated by social influences (the $qx(t) \cdot (1 - x(t))$ part of the equation) reached its maximum at exactly $x(t) = N(t)/2$. In other words, the social influences, which drive the contagion process, reach their maximal level many years in the future when half of the potential target market will have adopted the product.

4
Turning Points in the Product Life Cycle

The diffusion scenario deals with the evolution over time of a single market. Temporally, this process, as described by the Bass model, describes the market penetration of an innovation as a smooth curve, which increases monotonically until the entire market potential has adopted. This is a result of the assumptions behind the model which regard the social system as fully connected, and consider the innovation as standalone—without the influence of competition or influences by other markets and other technology generations of the product. However, in many real diffusion processes such influences are dominant, and the diffusion curve does not look as smooth and monotonic as described by the model. An exciting stream of research emerged in the past decade on turning points in the product life cycle that are not included in the classic smooth adoption curve (see illustration in Figure 5). In this chapter, we focus on research dealing with three turning points in the product life cycle: takeoff, which occurs at the beginning, saddle, which occurs during early growth, and

Figure 5
Turning Points in the Product Life Cycle

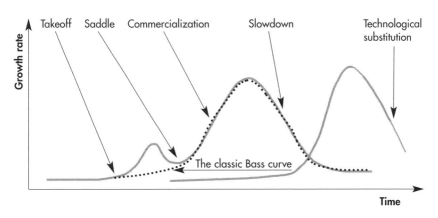

19

Table 2
Turning Points in the Product Life Cycle

Stage in Life Cycle	Main Research Focus	Paper	Data
Takeoff	Sources that influence time to takeoff	Golder and Tellis (1997)	31 U.S. innovations launched 1898–1990
		Agarwal and Bayus (2002)	30 U.S. innovations launched 1849–1984
		Tellis, Stremersch, and Yin (2003)	10 durables in 16 European countries
		Foster, Golder, and Tellis (2004)	40 U.S. innovations
		Goldenberg, Libai, and Muller (2010)	Fax machines, CB radios, CD players, and DVD players in the U.S.
Saddle	Saddle occurrence and its explanation as a dual-market phenomenon	Goldenberg, Libai, and Muller (2002)	32 U.S. consumer electronic innovations launched 1950–1985
		Muller and Yogev (2006)	35 U.S. consumer electronic innovations launched 1950
		Van den Bulte and Joshi (2007)	33 data sets of three categories: antibiotics, music CDs, high-tech products
Other turning points	Incubation time (the time between invention and launch)	Kohli, Lehmann, and Pae (1999)	32 U.S. durables in three categories, U.S., 1922–1992
	Commercialization, takeoff, and slowdown	Golder and Tellis (2004)	30 U.S. innovations launched 1929–1990

Results

Price

Market penetration

Entry of firms (a proxy for demand side)

Price decline

Demand-side explanation dominant

Region (Scandinavia faster than Mediterranean)

Product type (brown goods—CD, TV—take off faster)

Cultural factors (uncertainty avoidance and masculinity)

Later entry time (leads to shorter takeoffs)

Time frame (WWII, 1965, 1980)

Category

Price

Network externalities

A saddle exists in between 1/3 and 1/2 of the cases. Average relative depth is 25%, with duration of four years.

Saddle is created by cross-market communication gap.

Dual markets (early and main market) were reported in 26 of the 35 cases.

Average adoption at time wherein early and main market curves intersect is 16%.

A dual-market model can predict saddles.

Incubation time has a chilling effect on the p and q of the category.

Both diffusion and informational cascade were found to be significant. In the average sales figures, a saddle was observed.

technological substitution, which occurs at the late stages of growth. (A summary of literature on turning points in the life cycle is presented in Table 2.)

Takeoff

The classic Bass model starts with the spontaneous adoption of an initial seed of adopters. This is illustrated when we look at Equation 1 at time zero: if the initial conditions are $N(0) = 0$, then the number of new adopters at time zero, $dN(t)/dt$ is $p \cdot m$. The model does not provide explanations as to the mechanisms that led to this adoption. Studies on takeoff focus on this initial stage, and explore its market behavior and its interface with the start of communication interactions. The main tool used by researchers in this area is the proportional hazard model. We refer readers to the Appendix for the basic model structure, and to Bass, Jain, and Krishnan (2000), and Roberts and Lattin (2000) for elegant and exhaustive treatments of the adoption hazard function and its link to the Generalized Bass model.

The paper that took-off the literature on takeoff was that of Golder and Tellis from 1997. They defined the takeoff point as *the time at which a dramatic increase in sales occurs, that distinguishes the cutoff point between the introduction and growth stage of the product lifecycle.* In Figure 4 (page 16), which describes the penetration of mobile phones in Norway, this increase happened around 1985.

The importance of the takeoff time to the firm is clear: Rapid increase in sales requires substantial investments in production, distribution, and marketing, most of which require considerable lead time to be put into place successfully. Golder and Tellis (1997) apply a proportional hazard model on data that included 31 successful innovative product categories in the U.S. between 1898 (automobiles) and 1990 (direct broadcast satellite). They find that for post-WWII categories, the average time-to-takeoff is six years, and average penetration at takeoff is 1.7% of market potential. Price at takeoff is found to be 63% of original price.

The exact point of takeoff is not trivial to measure, since when penetration is very low a high percent change in sales (i.e., an increase from 1,000 to 2,000 subscribers of a mobile phone service) does not necessarily imply a takeoff. Golder and Tellis (1997), and later Agarwal and Bayus (2002) and Tellis, Stremersch, and Yin (2003), suggest methods for operationalizing this construct and measuring the time-to-takeoff. Such a method is to build a penetration threshold function, that is, to associate for each penetration level, the minimal percentage growth in sales which is required to be considered as takeoff. Figure

Figure 6
Threshold for Takeoff

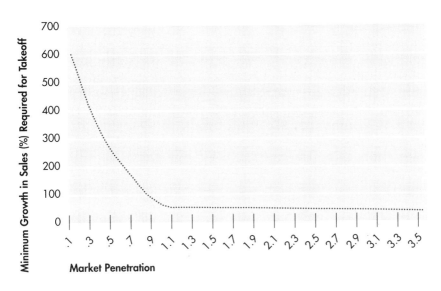

Market Penetration

(source: Tellis, Stremersch, and Yin 2003)

6 shows this threshold function which is commonly used (Tellis, Stremersch, and Yin 2003). For example, for a market penetration of 6%, market growth should be at least 200% for the point of time to be considered a takeoff. Of all the candidates for takeoff, the earliest year that satisfies this requirement is considered as the takeoff.

One should note that takeoff is a *sales* pattern phenomenon and not an *adoption* pattern. The two coincide when each customer adopts exactly one unit of the product and does not replace it over time. However, in the presence of multiple-unit purchases of a durable good by an adopter or repeat-purchase products and the like, sales are more meaningful units of analysis than adoption. For an excellent treatment of the subject, see Fader and Hardie (2001).

Some studies have investigated factors that influence the time-to-takeoff. Foster, Golder, and Tellis (2004) find, in a study of 40 innovative products, that the time-to-takeoff is influenced by price and product category. Tellis, Stremersch, and Yin (2003) inquire whether countries differ in the growth stage of diffusion, and examine the sources for these differences. They find that cultural factors have a positive effect on takeoff, but have less effect on duration of the growth phase. Surprisingly, economic wealth of a country has no effect on the takeoff time; it does, however, affect the time at which product sales begin to decline, with a resulting positive effect on duration of the growth phase.

A basic assumption of most studies is that takeoff is not generated by the internal dynamics of the market, and thus does not require any social influences. Rather, takeoff is seen as a result of external factors such as price, product type, and cultural heterogeneity. In our view, the takeoff point is the point of interface between external and internal influences. Although both exist along the entire diffusion process, external factors are more dominant before takeoff, and internal consumer interdependencies become more dominant after takeoff. It should be noted that takeoff studies to date are mostly descriptive, and there is a need for a comprehensive theory that dives deeper into the early market growth until the takeoff point.

In an attempt to further explore this interface, Goldenberg, Libai, and Muller (2010) investigate the effect of network externalities on the takeoff and speed of diffusion of innovative products. They assume that each individual in the market has a utility for the product, that is, a quantification of the total perceived net benefits that he or she can get from the product. As discussed in Chapter 2, for network goods such as fax or telephone, this utility might depend on the total number of adopters. Since people are heterogeneous, each has a personal threshold which determines the level of market penetration, in which this individual is ready to join the market potential and consider adoption. Using agent-based simulations and penetration data, Goldenberg, Libai, and Muller show that the higher the network effect (as measured by the mean of the threshold distribution), the slower is the time-to-takeoff. Hence, in early stages, network effects can substantially attenuate growth. Thus, the takeoff point is influenced by the interaction of customer heterogeneity and social influences.

Saddle

Following takeoff, the basic diffusion model predicts a monotonic increase in sales, up to the peak of growth. However, in some markets, this increase might be non-monotonic, and a sudden decrease in sales occurs after an initial rise. This was first observed by Geoffrey Moore, a Silicon Valley consultant (who denoted it as a "chasm"), and was later scientifically formalized and explored by Mahajan and Muller (1998), Goldenberg, Libai, and Muller (2002), Golder and

Tellis (2004), Muller and Yogev (2006), and Van den Bulte and Joshi (2007). Goldenberg, Libai, and Muller (2002) refer to this phenomenon as a saddle, and define it as a pattern in which *an initial peak predates a trough of sufficient depth and duration, followed by sales that eventually exceed the initial peak*.

While a saddle can be attributed to many causes, including stockpiling, changes in technology, industry performance, or macroeconomic events, it can be also explained by social influences.

Goldenberg, Libai, and Muller (2002) offer an explanation based on hetero-geneity in the adopting population and its division into two separate markets: an early market and main market. If these two markets adopt the innovation at widely differing rates, e.g., because of weak communication between the two, sales may show an intermediate trough. Muller and Yogev (2006) and Van den Bulte and Joshi (2007) show similar results when the market is divided into innovators and imitators. Both studies incorporate the idea of two markets into the classic equation: p_i and q_i and p_m and q_m represent external and internal coefficients of the early market and main market respectively. The cross-market communication between the early market and the main market is denoted by q_{im}, $x_i(t)$ is the percentage of adopters of the early market population, and $x_m(t)$ is the percentage of adopters of the main market population. The equations used by both studies can be written as:

$$\frac{dx_i(t)}{dt} = (p_i + q_i x_i(t)) \cdot (1 - x_i(t)) \tag{2a}$$

$$\frac{dx_m(t)}{dt} = (p_m + q_m x_m(t) + q_{im} x_i(t)) \cdot (1 - x_m(t)) \tag{2b}$$

Figure 7 illustrates the growth function described by these two equations applied on the growth data of corded phones (plain landline phones) in the U.S. from 1982 to 2000.

Equation 2 implies that saddle appears if p_m and q_m is considerably smaller than p_i and q_i and the cross-market communications (represented by q_{im}) are low enough. The above equations demonstrate how combining heterogeneity (in this case, the division to two markets) and social influences can explain a

Figure 7

Saddle in Diffusion of Corded Phones

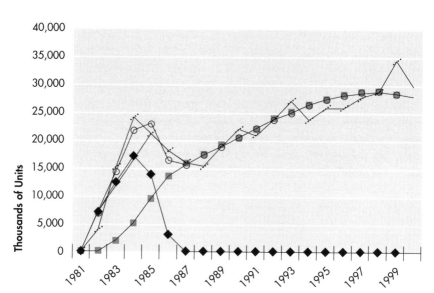

* The data start from 1981, although earlier technology generations date back to the 1870s.

phenomenon that deviates from the classical bell-shaped sales curve. However, these equations do not explain the nature of the interdependencies between the two markets; the parameter q_{im} might be a result of word-of-mouth, but it might also be the case that early market adoption serves as a signal (in this case, a discounted signal) to the adopters of the main market. Moreover, the basic issue of separating early and main market consumers from a behavioral point of view needs further study.

Technological Substitution

In theory, the diffusion process ends with the adoption of the product by the entire market potential. However, in practice, new products are often substituted with more advanced products and technological generations. New product growth across technology generations is occupying a growing interest among marketing scholars (e.g., Bass and Bass 2004, 2001; Mahajan and Muller 1996; Norton and Bass 1987, 1992). A summary of research on multi-generational diffusion can be found in Table 3.

The entry of a new technology generation complicates growth dynamics and generates consumer-related processes that are not found in single-generation diffusion. The entry of a new generation is usually considered to increase the market potential; in addition, customers can upgrade and substitute old technology with the new one. On the other hand, individuals who belong to the increased market potential might decide eventually to adopt the older generation, in which case they cannibalize the new technology's potential. If there are more than two generations, adopters might skip a generation and leapfrog to advanced versions. Surprisingly, no diffusion model offers a comprehensive treatment of these dynamics. Studies so far have focused on one or two of these aspects, such as upgrading (Bass and Bass 2004, 2001; Norton and Bass 1992) and cannibalization (Mahajan and Muller 1996), but a unified theoretical treatment of the subject is lacking.

Technological substitution raises some interesting questions about heterogeneity in the adopting population. Goldenberg and Oreg (2007) propose a redefinition of the laggards' concept, whereby laggards of previous product generations become the innovators of the latest generation because of leapfrogging. For example, in the early days of the MP3 revolution, an early adopter of MP3 could be a user of a Walkman cassette player who did not adopt CD and decided to upgrade by leapfrogging to MP3 player. Hence early adopters of MP3 are not necessarily innovative, but can be "leapfrogging laggards" from previous generations.

A major issue in these studies is whether the diffusion parameters change, or accelerate, between technology generations. This question has a practical importance for forecasting, particularly due to the need to forecast the growth of advanced generations in very early stages of their penetration, or even before launch. Theoretically, this question is important since it deals with dependency between a series of diffusion processes and, specifically, with development of the social system over time. Does the social system have memory, or does it start each diffusion process from scratch? If it has memory, how strong is it? How deep back in time does it reach?

As Stremersch, Muller, and Peres (2009) point out, the literature offers contradictory answers to these questions. Several studies across multiple product categories find that growth parameters are constant across technology generations (Bayus 1994; Bass and Bass 2004; Kim, Chang, and Shocker 2000; Mahajan and Muller 1996; Norton and Bass 1992, 1987). Bayus (1998) uses a

Table 3
Multi-generational Diffusion

Paper	Data
Bayus (1998)	Four generations of PC computers from 1974 to 1992 world-wide, for 20 manufacturers
Kim, Chang, and Shocker (2000)	Three categories: pagers, two generations of cell phones, and CT2 in Korea, 1984–1994
Mahajan and Muller (1996)	Four generations of IBM mainframe computers, 1955–1978
Norton and Bass (1992)	Up to four generations of six electronic products, three pharmaceuticals, two consumer goods, and one industrial good, 1960–1987
Pae and Lehmann (2003)	45 generations in 15 product categories, 1868–1994
Stremersch, Muller, and Peres (2009)	41 generations in 13 product categories

proportional hazard model on four generations of PCs to conclude that the average product life is not declining over time, even when moderating variables (such as year of entry and technology used) are included. The few exceptions to these consistent findings are found by Islam and Meade (1997) and Pae and Lehmann (2003) who show acceleration of the diffusion parameters. Their findings are challenged by Van den Bulte (2004), who demonstrates that their results can be an artifact of the difference in the lengths of the data series used in the analysis.

Challenging the assumption of stability of parameters across generations, there is massive evidence that in general, diffusion processes of recent product categories are faster than diffusion processes of older categories (Kohli,

Intergenerational Process	Acceleration?
The lifetime duration of a product from introduction to peak of sales is a function of the firm's year of entry and the technology.	No acceleration in generational lifetime duration
Adopter groups: new buyers and upgraders Market potential increases with generation.	No acceleration in p and q Similarity in growth rate between product categories
Adopter groups: new buyers, upgraders, cannibals, and leapfroggers Market potential increases with generation.	No acceleration in p and q
Adopter groups: new buyers and upgraders Market potential increases with generation.	No acceleration in p and q
Adopter groups: Only new buyers for each generation; generations develop independently. Market potential increases with generation.	The larger is the entry time difference between generations, the lower are the p and q of the new generation.
Adopter groups: New buyers, upgraders, cannibals. Market potential increases with generation.	Acceleration in time-to-takeoff Takeoff acceleration is due to vintage effect and not to technological substitution.

Lehmann, and Pae 1999; Van den Bulte 2000, 2002; Agarwal and Bayus 2002; Van den Bulte and Stremersch 2004, 2008; Chandrasekaran and Tellis 2008). Van den Bulte (2000) investigates the issue of acceleration by taking the Bass model with the external influence (p) set to zero, and running the model on 31 product categories in consumer electronics and household products. The average annual acceleration between 1946 and 1980 is found to be around 2%. Exceptions to this generalized finding are rare (Bayus 1994) and contested on the grounds of estimation bias and invalid inference (Van den Bulte 2000).

Clearly, these two research streams, one finding stable growth parameters across generations, the other finding acceleration of diffusion of product categories over time, form an intriguing paradox: It is clear that in the same

Figure 8
Sales Evolution of Two Generations of Home Entertainment

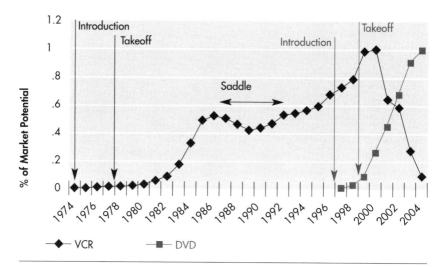

economy, an acceleration of diffusion processes over time should be reflected in acceleration of technology generations that succeed each other. A resolution to this seeming inconsistency is suggested by Stremersch, Muller, and Peres (2009), who investigate whether the faster growth of successive generations is due to the passage of time or to the generational effect. They define *technology generation* as a set of products similar in customer-perceived characteristics, and *technology vintage* as the year in which the first model of a specific technology generation was launched commercially. Using a discrete proportional hazard model on 41 generations in 13 product categories, Stremersch, Muller, and Peres find that acceleration is observed only in time-to-takeoff but not in the diffusion parameters, which describe the overall process. They also find that the takeoff acceleration is due to passage of time and not to generational shifts. Thus, time indeed accelerates early growth, but generational shifts do not.

To summarize our discussion on turning points, Figure 8 displays the sales evolution—introduction, takeoffs, saddle, and substitution—of two successive generations in home entertainment, namely VCR and DVD, in which sales have been normalized between 0 and 1. As it illustrates, in the home entertainment market, sales of the second generation (DVD) took off faster than the sales of the first generation (VCR). However, comparing the general slope of the two curves indicates a similar growth rate. Also, the sales of the first generation (VCR) showed a saddle, while the second generation (DVD) did not.

5
Spatial Effects in Diffusion of Innovations

Diffusion of an innovation occurs in space as well as in time. Spatial aspects are important since they may reveal social influences that go beyond word-of-mouth communications. For example, the adoption processes of consumers in different geographical areas can influence each other even without direct communication, through signals and network externalities. In addition, location-derived characteristics (such as culture and wealth) can help explain heterogeneity between different social systems and its influences in the adoption process. The spatial dimensions of diffusion become especially important in multi-market growth, as in a large country such as the U.S. or in international penetration of a new product.

Here, we discuss briefly the issue of spatial diffusion and then focus on multinational diffusion—we review the differences in the growth patterns across countries and their drivers, as well as strategies for multi-market introduction of new products.

Research dealing directly with spatial effects in diffusion is not ubiquitous. Traditionally, diffusion models did not incorporate spatial interactions: Their assumption was that the social system is uniformly connected and that social influences are not affected by spatial location. Most studies in spatial marketing discuss issues in retailing, and do not involve social influences (e.g., Bronnenberg and Mela 2004; Bronnenberg and Mahajan 2001; Bronnenberg, Mahajan, and Vanhonacker 2000; Allaway et al. 1994).

The main research question one might ask is, Does the additional information conveyed by the spatial aspects of the diffusion process help in better predicting its course? For example, given eight quarters' worth of sales data, broken down by sales territories, can one predict the next couple of quarters better than if the data were given in the aggregate without the territorial breakdown? This question is still unanswered. A first attempt to answer this question was done by Garber et al. (2004), who predict the success or failure of a product based on the initial spatial distribution of adopters. They claim that since word-of-mouth spread is often associated with some level of geographical proximity

Table 4
Multinational Diffusion: Cross-country Influences

Paper	Data
Elberse and Eliashberg (2003)	164 films Domestic: U.S.; foreign: France, Germany, Spain
Ganesh, Kumar, and Subramaniam (1997)	Four durables, 15 European countries tested in pairs
Eliashberg and Helsen (1996)	VCRs in 13 European countries, sales data of a single firm
Ganesh and Kumar (1996)	B2B durables: supermarket scanners in U.S., Japan, and eight European countries
Kumar and Krishnan (2002)	Case studies of three durables in 6 European countries, tested in pairs
Putsis et al. (1997)	Four durables in products, 10 European countries
Van Everdingen, Aghina, and Fok (2005)	Internet access, landline, and cellular telephony in 15 European countries

between the parties involved, one can expect that the beginning of a successful diffusion process will be expressed in the formation of "clusters". The absence of such clusters indicates a possible failure of the product.

Cross-country Influences

A growing number of papers since 1990 address the increasing importance of multinational product acceptance, and extend the traditional single market scope of the Bass model to explore problems and issues related to international diffusion (Dekimpe, Parker, and Sarvary 2000a).

A key issue in multinational diffusion is the *mutual influences* of diffusion processes across countries. One of the major findings of the studies on cross-country influences is that entry time lag has a positive influence on the diffusion process, that is, countries that introduce a given innovation later show a

Findings

1. Domestic performance influences foreign availability and revenues.
2. This influence decreases with the time lag between domestic and foreign launches. The cross-country effect is influenced by cultural and economic similarity, continuous/radical innovation, existence of standards, and entry time lag. It is not affected by geographic proximity!

1. Most cross-country influence is smaller than within-country influence, and might be negative.
2. The influence goes from big countries to small countries.
Cross-country influence δ is positive and significant.

Influences exist in all directions: lead lag, lag lead, and simultaneous.

Countries with strong influence on other countries should be the first to begin with.

Using dynamic parameters provides better fit and forecast.

faster diffusion process (Tellis, Stremersch, and Yin 2003; Dekimpe, Parker, and Sarvary 2000b, 2000c; Ganesh, Kumar, and Subramaniam 1997; Takada and Jain 1991), and a faster time-to-takeoff (Van Everdingen, Fok, and Stremersch 2009). This cross-country influence is occasionally termed *lead-lag effect*; however, influence can also be multi-directional. Taking exception to this finding are studies by Desiraju, Nair, and Chintagunta (2004) and Elberse and Eliashberg (2003).

A sound body of papers models multi-market diffusion with cross-country influences (e.g., Ganesh, Kumar, and Subramaniam 1997; Putsis et al. 1997; Eliashberg and Helsen 1996). Table 4 offers a summary of this research. Generalizing over the models used in these studies, a generic cross-country influence model may take the following form; ($x_i(t)$ is the proportion of adopters in country i at time t):

$$\frac{dx_i(t)}{dt} = (p_i + q_i x_i(t) + \sum_{j \neq i} \delta_{ij} x_j(t)) \cdot (1 - x_i(t)) \tag{3}$$

The influence matrix δ_{ij} represents the cross-country effects between a country i and another country j. It can be interpreted as representing two types of influence mechanisms: weak ties and signals. Weak ties come from adopters of one country who communicate with non-adopters from other countries (Wuyts et al. 2004; Rindfleisch and Moorman 2001). However, even without communicating or imitating other individuals, non-adopters are influenced by the diffusion in other countries. In other words, the level of acceptance of the innovation in one country acts as a *signal* for customers in other countries, reducing their perception of risk and increasing the legitimacy of using the new product. While several studies state explicitly that the dominant cross-country influence is word-of-mouth communication (Putsis et al. 1997; Eliashberg and Helsen 1996; Ganesh and Kumar 1996), others explore cross-country effect without reference to the specific mechanism (e.g., Dekimpe, Parker, and Sarvary 2000b, 2000c; Takada and Jain 1991).

Although the distinction between weak ties and signals has evident managerial implications, the commonly used aggregate models of the type presented in Equation 3 do not distinguish between the two; both are represented through the parameters δ_{ij}. Further research is required to estimate the relative role of word-of-mouth and signals on cross-country spillover and to study their relative effects on the overall diffusion process.

As we discuss in Chapter 8, individual-level models might be able to make this distinction. However, this is not a trivial task, due to the difficulty of converting individual-level models to aggregate models and the need to construct the estimation procedure.

Only a limited number of studies have explored multinational diffusion with the aim of informing managerial decision making to optimize the diffusion process. Some studies explore entry strategy, i.e., should a firm enter all its markets simultaneously (a "sprinkler" strategy), or sequentially (a "waterfall" strategy)? Kalish, Mahajan, and Muller (1995) model a game for two brands in the home market and imply that when conditions in foreign markets are unfavorable (slow growth or low innovativeness), competitive pressure is low, the lead-lag effect is high, and fixed entry costs are high, a waterfall strategy is preferred. Libai, Muller, and Peres (2005) extend this question to explore responsive budgeting strategies, where firms dynamically allocate their marketing efforts according to developments in the market. Other issues such as regulation, international competition, and optimal marketing mix of international growing markets need to be further explored and studied.

Table 5
Sources for Differences in Diffusion Parameters

Source	Parameter	Influence
Entry time	Entry time lag	Mostly positive
Marketing mix	Price	Mixed
	Product type	Positive (Brown goods, CD Players, TVs, camcorders, etc., penetrate faster.)
Market related	Existence of competition	Positive
	Regulation	Positive
Demographic and cultural	Population heterogeneity	Negative
	Population growth rate	Positive
	Number of population centers	Mixed
	Hofstede (2001) dimensions	Positive Direction: less uncertainly avoidance, collectivism, masculinity, and power distance enhance diffusion.
Economic	Wealth (GDP, income per capita)	Positive
	Media availability	Mixed
	Income inequality	Positive

Differences in Growth Patterns across Countries

The research on the evolution of multi-markets reveals a noteworthy aspect of diffusion which deals with heterogeneity between different social systems in adopting the same product. During the last two decades, a large number of studies have focused on describing and explaining inter-country differences; key findings are summarized in Table 5. These studies usually focus on the differences in the diffusion parameters p and/or q (e.g., Van den Bulte 2002; Dekimpe, Parker, and Sarvary 1998; Helsen, Jedidi, and DeSarbo 1993; Takada and Jain 1991), the ratio of q/p (Van den Bulte and Stremersch 2004), time-to-takeoff (Tellis, Stremersch, and Yin 2003), and duration of the growth stage (Stremersch and Tellis 2004).

As Table 5 demonstrates, diffusion processes vary greatly between countries, even for the same products, and even within the same continent (Ganesh 1998; Mahajan and Muller 1994; Helsen, Jedidi, and DeSarbo 1993). In addition to measuring the differences, many studies also investigate the country-specific sources that generate differences in the growth process. In addition to entry time, discussed above, these factors can be divided into *cultural* sources, *economic* sources, and *market-related* sources.

Cultural Sources Cultural sources relate to the country's cultural characteristics and values. Takada and Jain (1991) find that the diffusion parameter q is higher in countries that are high-context and homophilous, such as Asian-Pacific countries, relative to countries such as the U.S., which are low-context and heterophilous, where *high-context* refers to a culture where much of a communication's information resides in its context as opposed to the explicit message, and *homophilous* implies that communication takes place among similar individuals. Similarly, Dekimpe, Parker, and Sarvary find that regarding cellular phones (2000b) and industrial digital telephone switches (2000c), population heterogeneity has a negative effect on both the time to adoption and on the transition probability between non-adoption to partial and full adoption in a country. A similar finding is described in Talukdar, Sudhir, and Ainslie (2002).

Dwyer, Mesak, and Hsu (2005) use Hofstede's dimensions of national culture[1] and find a positive relationship between q and collectivism (vs. individualism), masculinity, and high power distance. Their findings are also supported by Van den Bulte and Stremersch (2004). Also, short-term orientation is positively associated with q; interestingly, in their data, Dwyer, Mesak, and Hsu do not find a significant negative relationship to uncertainty avoidance.

Economic Sources The influences of many macroeconomic variables have been studied, yielding two main empirical generalizations: First, the wealth of the country (usually measured by GDP per capita, but also by lifestyle, health status, and urbanization) has a positive influence on diffusion (Desiraju, Nair, and Chintagunta 2004; Talukdar, Sudhir, and Ainslie 2002; Dekimpe, Parker, and Sarvary 2000b, 2000c; Putsis et al. 1997; Helsen, Jedidi, and DeSarbo 1993). Note that wealth does not necessarily mean general welfare, i.e., Van den Bulte and Stremersch (2004) find a positive influence between the Gini index for inequality, and the ratio q/p. This finding is consistent with the cultural findings concerning the positive associations with power distance and masculinity.

A second generalization is that access to mass media (usually operationalized by the penetration of TV sets) has a positive influence on diffusion parameter p (Stremersch and Tellis 2004; Talukdar, Sudhir, and Ainslie 2002; Tellefsen and Takada 1999; Putsis et al. 1997). In pharmaceutical markets, regulation is also found to influence growth in sales (Stremersch and Lemmens 2009). Tellis, Stremersch, and Yin (2003) and Stremersch and Tellis (2004) distinguish between the influences of cultural and economic factors on the penetration stages; they find that cultural factors influence time-to-takeoff, while economic factors influence growth.

Market-related Sources All of the above factors relate to country characteristics. However, it is reasonable to assume that factors related to the market structure in a given country—such as regulation, competition, and price levels—will also affect the diffusion. Only a few studies have investigated market–related sources. Regarding *competition,* evidence is mixed. Dekimpe, Parker, and Sarvary (1998) find that competition is positively associated with the parameter p. This finding is supported by Kauffman and Techatassanasoontorn (2005), who show that the diffusion rate is enhanced by the existence of competing technologies; and by Van den Bulte and Stremersch (2004), who find in a meta-analysis on the variation on q/p, a positive influence on the existence of competing standards. In contradiction, Dekimpe, Parker, and Sarvary (2000c) show a negative effect of existing installed base in the old technology on the growth process.

Despite the large number of studies on differences between countries, two necessary steps are needed to complete the puzzle. First, research so far indicates the sources for variation, but not the way in which they influence the diffusion parameters. Second, data so far should be extended to include a larger variety of countries, including developing countries (Mahajan and Banga 2006). In particular, we would like to know whether the same patterns and the same forces are at work in developing countries as in developed countries, or if the theories have to be revised.

Note

1. Hofstede's dimensions of natural culture are defined as (Hofstede 2001): *uncertainty avoidance*—the extent to which the members of a culture feel threatened by uncertain or unknown situations; *individualism vs. collectivism*—the degree to which the interests of the group prevail over those of the individual; *masculinity vs. femininity*—traditional, stereotypical, gender roles of society in which assertiveness and competitiveness define masculinity and nurturing, caring, and focus on quality of life distinguish femininity; *power distance*—the extent to which the less powerful members of institutions and organizations in a country expect and accept that power is distributed unequally.

6
Diffusion and Competition

Competitive forces influence the growth and decision making for many new products. Although some innovative categories start as monopolies, many of them quickly develop to include multiple competing brands. Interestingly, the existence of competition not only influences the interactions of customers with the firms, but also influences the dynamics of the interactions of consumers with other consumers. Thus, a competitive growing market reveals a range of social influences that are not present in a monopoly: word-of-mouth can be exchanged within and between brands, compatibility issues can increase or decrease the effect of network externalities, and the entry of a new competitor can form a signal as to the quality of the product.

Figure 9 illustrates various competitive effects that modify and influence the growth process and that do not exist in monopolies. These competitive effects relate to customer flow and information flow. Regarding customer flow, the firms compete in a double frontier—first is acquisition of adopters from the market potential before their competitors, and second is acquisition and loss of customers who churn. Their competitors might be legal brands, or illegal brands, hence a third frontier of coping with piracy is also at play. The information flow under competition becomes more complex since consumers' communication exists within and between brands. Among these effects are the influences of competition on the category growth rate, and communication transfer within and between brands.

Despite the richness of these phenomena, the traditional diffusion literature deals either with growth of monopolies or with category-level growth. The literature on competition has investigated mature markets, and fewer studies have focused on competitive effects in growing markets (see Chatterjee, Eliashberg, and Rao 2000 for review). Only in the last two decades do we see papers that combine the diffusion stream with the competition literature and add some of the competitive effects into diffusion modeling; we will review some of them in this chapter and in Table 6.

A preliminary question in the discussion of competition and diffusion is whether competition enhances or delays category growth. Generally, competi-

Figure 9
Competitive Effects on Focal Brand A of Competition for Market Potential, Piracy, Cross-brand Communication, and Churning Customers to and from Competitors

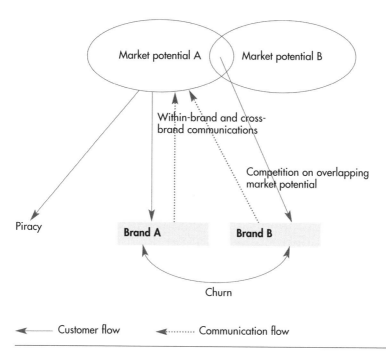

tion is found to have a positive effect on diffusion parameters (Kauffman and Techatassanasoontorn 2005; Van den Bulte and Stremersch 2004; Kim, Bridges, and Srivastava 1999; Dekimpe, Parker, and Sarvary 1998). An exception is found in Dekimpe, Parker, and Sarvary (2000c) who show a negative effect of an existing installed base of the old technology on the growth process. Krishnan, Bass, and Kumar (2000) study the impact of late entrants on the diffusion of incumbent brands. Testing on minivans and cellular phones in U.S. states, they find that the effect varies across markets: In some markets, the market potential and the internal communication parameter q increase with the entry of an additional brand, while in other markets, only one of them increases with competition entry. None of these studies explains the mechanisms behind the acceleration. Is it a result of a higher marketing pressure on the target market? Is the number of competitors a signal to the quality and long-term potential of the product (as implicitly suggested by Kim, Bridges, and Srivastava 1999)? Or is the positive effect a result of reduction in network externalities (Van den Bulte and Stremersch 2004)? Further research is still needed here.

In order to model competitive markets, the diffusion framework was extended from describing a monopoly or a category, to describing the growth of a brand. Constructing such a brand-growth model involves several conceptual issues. A basic question is, To what extent are the diffusion mechanisms of external and internal influence we discussed in the basic Bass monopoly model valid also at the brand level? Some argue they are not. Such approaches regard adoption as a two-stage process, where adopters first adopt the category and then choose the brand through external factors such as promotion activities, price deals, and special offers (Givon, Mahajan, and Muller 1995; Hahn et al. 1994). In spite of the intuitive rational of this approach, it is almost never used, partially because it requires high-quality individual-level data. The development of service markets and the increased use of CRM systems by service providers can facilitate data availability and promote usage of these types of models. For example, Landsman and Givon (2009) use banking data to investigate growth of financial products; Weerahandi and Dalal (1992) use business-to-business data for fax penetration.

Although the exact mechanisms of brand-level versus category-level adoption are not clear yet, the main body of literature assumes that communications apply also at the brand level, and therefore a Bass-type model can be used to model choice. If so, what is the nature of the internal communication between adopters and the remaining market potential? Basically, a potential customer joins brand i as an outcome of *within-brand* communication with the adopters of brand i, or *cross-brand communication* with adopters of other brands. A consumer's adopting a brand can occur due to negative information on competing brands, or to the consumer receiving information about the category from the other brands' adopters, yet finding brand i's marketing mix more appealing. Generalizing over the competitive diffusion models published so far, a diffusion equation for multiple brands that explicitly presents both communication paths (adapted from Libai, Muller, and Peres 2009a; Savin and Terwiesch 2005) can take this form:

$$\frac{dN_i(t)}{dt} = \left(p_i + q_i \frac{N_i(t)}{m} + \sum_{j \neq i} \delta_{ij} \frac{N_j(t)}{m}\right) \cdot (m - N(t)) \tag{4}$$

Table 6
Diffusion Models: Brand Level and Competition Issues

Competitive Effect	Paper	Research Question
Influence of competition	Hahn et al. (1994)	The influence of competition on customer trial and repeat purchase
	Kim, Bridges, and Srivastava (1999)	The influence of number of competitors and market entries/exits on category growth
Early/late entry	Krishnan, Bass, and Kumar (2000)	The influence of a late entrant on diffusion
Within-brand and cross-brand influences	Parker and Gatignon (1994)	Within- and cross-brand word-of-mouth during diffusion
	Libai, Muller, and Peres (2009a)	The influence of within-brand and cross-brand communications on competitive growth
Competition for market potential	Mahajan, Sharma, and Buzzell (1993)	Kodak and Polaroid competitive scope
Churn	Libai, Muller, and Peres (2009b)	The influence of churn on the growth of services
Piracy	Givon, Mahajan, and Muller (1995)	Software piracy and its impact on diffusion
	Prasad and Mahajan (2003)	What is the optimum level of piracy that a firm should tolerate?
Churn + piracy	Givon, Mahajan, and Muller (1997)	The net effect of brand switching and piracy on user-based share and unit sales-based share

Data	Results
Pharmaceuticals	Repeat purchase depends on competition and product characteristics.
Video cassettes, personal computers, and workstations	1. Market potential and external influence increase with the number of competitors. 2. The dependence of entries on number of competitors is complex, and might depend on whether or not a "shakeout" occurred in the market. 3. Exits increase with number of competitors.
Minivans and cellular phones in various states of the U.S.	The market potential, q_i, or both increase after entry.
Data on sales of nine brands of hair-styling mousse	For some brands, there is significant cross-brand communication.
Cellular markets in Europe	The ratio of the cross- to within-brand influences determines the existence, size, and sustainability of the pioneering advantage.
Digital cameras: An old brand (pack) and a new brand (integral) of Polaroid vs. a new brand of Kodak	1. Polaroid pack developed mainly its own potential market. 2. Kodak took ~30% of its customers from Polaroid's potential buyers. 3. Kodak expanded the market for Polaroid.
Five service industries	Attrition influences the effective market potential and the time to maximum growth.
Spreadsheet software and word processors in the U.K.	Piracy has an enhancing effect on diffusion.
Theoretical	For the competitive case, the optimal tolerance of piracy is higher than in monopoly.
Two brands of spreadsheet software and word processors in the U.K.	Piracy and brand switching have inverse influences on user-based market share and unit sales-based market share respectively. The net effect works in both directions.

where $N(t)$ is the total number of adopters $(N(t) = \sum_j N_j(t))$, and δ_{ij} represents the cross-brand influences.

Most of the existing brand-level diffusion models are special cases or variations on this generic model. Some assume that within-brand communication equals that of the cross-brand, namely $\delta_{ij} = q_i$ (Krishnan, Bass, and Kumar 2000; Kim, Bridges, and Srivastava 1999; Kalish, Mahajan, and Muller 1995). Their underlying assumption is that there is no relevance to the brand ownership of the individual who spreads the information. Other models, such as that of Mahajan, Sharma, and Buzzell (1993), assume that the entire communications are brand specific.

The relationship between the Bass model and the summation of the equations of individual brands in each category should be further studied. For example, when $\delta_{ij} = q_i$, summing the equations for all brands yields the category equation of the Bass model; however, when cross-brand communication is not equal to within-brand, the summation results are otherwise. Two studies tried to examine systematically the distinction between within- and cross-brand communications: Parker and Gatignon (1994) and Libai, Muller, and Peres (2009a). Measuring consumer goods (Parker and Gatignon) and cellular services (Libai, Muller and Peres), they conclude that both within- and cross-brand influences exist.

Note the formative resemblance between Equation 4 and Equation 3 in the previous chapter: both describe spillover of social influences. However, Equation 3 represents influences of consumers from other markets, while Equation 4 deals with influences from customers of competing firms. As argued above, δ_{ij} can represent any type of influence, and further research is needed to separate the various effects of word-of-mouth, signals, and network externalities.

A conceptual difference between the two equations relates to the market potential. The multinational Equation 3 describes diffusion processes that operate in separate markets, where each process draws from its own market potential. In the competitive scenario of Equation 4, the assumption is that both firms compete on the same market potential. Some studies relax the assumption of a joint potential and assume that brands can develop independently, where each brand has its own market potential (Parker and Gatignon 1994); in this case, the market potential m in Equation 4 should be modified to m_i, i.e., the equation should now be:

$$\frac{dN_i(t)}{dt} = \left(p_i + \frac{q_i\, N_i(t)}{m_i} + \sum_{j \neq i} \delta_{ij} \frac{N_j(t)}{m_j} \right) \cdot (m_i - N_i(t)) \tag{5}$$

Note that Equation 5 requires a careful treatment and interpretation. If one assumes that the market potentials of the brands do not overlap with each other, then the brands do not compete for the attention and wallets of the same potential consumers. On the other hand, if one assumes that the markets potentials of the brands do overlap, and the total market potential $m = \sum m_j$, then this overall market potential overestimates the actual market potential, as the intersections should be subtracted from the overall count.

Mahajan, Sharma, and Buzzell (1993) investigate the market potential issue through the lawsuit of Polaroid against Kodak, in which the latter was accused of patent violation and attracting Polaroid's prospective customers to a new brand of digital camera. By breaking the non-adopter pool $(m - N(t))$ into sub-pools, according to the market potential of each brand, and estimating the parameters, they concluded that Kodak took about 30% of its customers from Polaroid's potential buyers. However, at the same time, Kodak expanded the market for Polaroid, since over 2/3 of Polaroid's sales would not have occurred if Kodak had not entered the market.

In addition to competition for market potential, in repeat-purchase products such as consumer goods or services, firms can compete for each other's existing customers. Brand switching, also termed *attrition, defection,* or *churn,* is a major concern in many innovative industries. For example, in the U.S. mobile industry, the average annual churn rate for 2005 is estimated at 26.2% (WCIS database), while the average attrition rate in U.S. companies is estimated at 20% (80% retention) (Reichheld 1996). Attrition and its consequences in mature markets are discussed in the CRM literature. However, recent studies demonstrate that customer attrition can have a substantial effects in growing markets (Gupta, Lehmann, and Stuart 2004; Hogan, Lemon, and Libai 2003; Thompson and Sinha 2008). Unfortunately, only a small number of studies attempts to incorporate churn into the diffusion framework (Libai, Muller, and Peres 2009b; Givon, Mahajan, and Muller 1997; Hahn et al. 1994).

7

Effects of Pricing and Advertising

Firms' activities and their investments in marketing have a considerable influence on the growth process of a new product, directly, through the customer's benefits from the innovation, as well as indirectly, through the three types of social influences. Increasing price, for example, can generate positive or negative word-of-mouth, can be a signal for quality or scarcity, and can also, in some cases, influence network externalities, as in the case of interconnectivity fees in the cellular industry. In this chapter, we review growth with marketing mix variables, specifically, the effects of pricing and advertising.

The diffusion literature in the 1980s dedicated efforts to marketing mix questions; particularly vis-à-vis optimal advertising and pricing over time (see Bass, Jain, and Krishnan 2000 for review). Research since then has focused on descriptive and normative research questions, primarily addressing price and advertising. A list of studies dealing with diffusion and marketing mix is summarized in Table 7.

One of the major criticisms of the Bass model is that it does not contain marketing mix variables, hence it does not enable managers to forecast the consequences of their marketing mix decisions on the growth of the new product. In 1994, Bass, Krishnan, and Jain introduced the Generalized Bass model (GBM), which assumes that the effect of the marketing mix variables vector $z(t)$ can be described by a non-negative function $\phi(z(t))$ that multiplies the basic curve as follows:

$$\frac{dx(t)}{dt} = (p + qx\,(t)) \cdot (1 - x(t))\phi(z(t)) \tag{6}$$

The authors assume a specific functional form in which the marketing mix, and specifically advertising and pricing, are measured as percent change rather than absolute values. When the percentage change in price and advertising is constant, $\phi(z(t))$ is constant, and the GBM reduces to the original Bass model. The authors test several categories of durable goods, and find that constant rate change is a reasonable assumption, which explains why the original Bass model

Table 7
Diffusion Models: Marketing Mix Decisions

Marketing Mix Variable	Paper	Research Question
Price	Krishnan, Bass, and Jain (1999)	Optimal pricing strategies for new products using the Generalized Bass model
	Mesak and Darrat (2002)	Optimal pricing of services in a market with service providers and consumers
	Lehmann and Esteban-Bravo (2006)	Should a firm subsidize its early adopters to speed adoption?
Price of successive generations	Bayus (1992)	Optimal pricing for successive generations (Switching to the second generation is done either by replacement when the product is worn out, or by upgrading.)
	Padmanabhan and Bass (1993)	Optimal pricing of successive technological generations
	Danaher, Hardie, and Putsis (2001)	The effect of price on the diffusion of technological generations; dual price structure: first-time purchase and subscription renewal
Advertising	Feichtinger (1992)	What is the diffusion pattern under the "constant percentage of advertising to sales" rule?
	Mesak (1996)	Optimal advertising
	Libai, Muller, and Peres (2005)	Dispersion vs. focus of marketing efforts in international entry

Data	Results
Theoretical	1. For high price sensitivity and high discount rate, the optimal price is monotonically decreasing over time. 2. For lower price sensitivity and discount rate, optimal price has a ceiling.
Optimal control	When discount rate is high (myopic industry), optimal price decreases with time. For low discount rate, optimal price increases with time.
Theoretical	In many cases, it is logical to subsidize innovators, main market, or both. When inter-segment influence is very weak, there is no point in subsidizing.
Theory + empirical support from durable goods sales data	1. For upgrading only, optimal price decreases for second generation and increases for first generation. 2. For on-time replacement only, optimal price decreases for both generations.
Theory	When generations belong to different firms, the optimal price for the first generation is higher than when they belong to the same firm. Price of second generation is equal between scenarios.
Cellular penetration in a European country, two generations	1. A price decrease of second generation increases its demand, yet decreases demand for first generation. 2. A price decrease of first generation increases both its sales and sales of second generation.
Theoretical	Adoption moves periodically between low and high customer numbers, depending on the interplay between acquisition and loss of customers.
U.S. cable TV	For static price, distribution, and advertising elasticities, optimal advertising is a percentage of sales.
Formal analysis and cellular automata simulations	Dispersing marketing efforts yields faster penetration. Moderators: entry costs, level of responsiveness to advertising

Table 7 (continued)
Marketing Mix Decisions

Marketing Mix Variable	Paper	Research Question
Product	Jain, Mahajan, and Muller (1991)	How do supply restrictions affect new product growth?
Distribution channels	Jones and Ritz (1991)	Incorporating distribution into the diffusion model
	Lehmann and Weinberg (2000)	Optimal entry time of a channel introduced second in a sequence (e.g., movies and video release); video entry time to maximize joint profits

provides a high fit and forecasting even without marketing mix variables. Studies that followed the GBM compare its performance to that of the original Bass model and their general conclusion is that both models provide a similar fit (Karine, Frank, and Laine 2004; Danaher, Hardie, and Putsis 2001; Bottomley and Fildes 1998). Krishnan, Seetharaman, and Vakratsas (2007) extend the GBM to brand-level analysis and use data on SUV buyers at the brand as well as category level.

The GBM has two main limitations: First, when $z(t)$ depends on the change of the elements of the marketing mix, it means that a constant budget, or a constant price, will not influence the growth function, an outcome that is counterintuitive to business practice. The second limitation is that the marketing mix variables have an equal effect on the internal and external (p and q) components of the model. This assumption is at odds with earlier work that models advertising as affecting only the external coefficient, and also with later results of Feichtinger (1992) and Mesak (1996); however, it is very much consistent with pricing assumptions such as those of Robinson and Lakhani (1975), who use a multiplicative model based on the same assumption. There is room for further research on the GBM in terms of diagnostic issues such as optimal marketing mix or understanding nonstandard growth patterns. In addition, the influence of marketing mix variables on each type of consumer interaction—word-of-mouth, signals, and network externalities—should be studied.

Data	Results
Applicants and subscribers for telephone service in Israel, 1949–1987	Supply constraints bring about negatively skewed diffusion patterns; the waiting list creates negative word-of-mouth.
Movie-goers and theater owners in the U.S.	Two levels of adopters: retailers (adopt through a Bass-type process); consumers (a fixed adoption rate). Each retailer opens the market to k consumers.
35 films in the U.S.: movie and video release	Assumption: Video release brings down movie sales. Tradeoff: Early video entry leads to higher video revenues, lower film revenues. Movies are released to video later than the optimal.

Decisions on marketing mix variables become more complex as heterogeneity is considered. An interesting example is discussed by Lehmann and Esteban-Bravo (2006), who explore the influence of consumer heterogeneity on optimal pricing. Specifically, they use a variation on the GBM to investigate the question of whether and how a firm should subsidize its early adopters in order to enhance adoption. Their conclusion demonstrates the direct negative effect of the level of heterogeneity; as long as communication between adopter categories exceeds a certain level, subsidizing early adopters is worthwhile for the firm.

A fascinating group of studies ties pricing decisions to the interdependency between consumers in subsequent technological generations. In a descriptive study on the cellular industry in Europe, Danaher, Hardie, and Putsis (2001) find an interesting interaction between generations in the response to price: A price decrease for generation 2 increases demand, yet also decreases the demand for generation 1. However, a price decrease for generation 1 increases both its sales as well as the sales of generation 2, since the users of generation 1 are a subset of the potential for later generations. Other studies in this spirit are performed by Bayus (1992), and Padmanabhan and Bass (1993). The latter adds inter-firm dependency when comparing a case in which both generations belong to the same firm, to the case in which each generation is produced by a different firm. They find that in the competitive case, the price for the first generation is higher than the price in the case of a single firm. In both cases, the price of the second generation is the same.

Little research attention has focused on the other two elements of marketing mix, namely product and distribution channels. Empirical evidence indicates that product characteristics have an influence on growth pattern (Henard and Szymanski 2001; Mishra, Kim, and Lee 1996; Rogers 1995). Tellis, Stremersch, and Yin (2003) find that brown goods take off faster than do white goods. However, these studies are descriptive by nature; they do not examine the processes through which product decisions affect the social influences that eventually lead to adoption. For example, a firm might decide to make its products compatible to reduce network externalities. Alternatively, it might use certain technology as a signal to the market, as in the mid 1990s, when many software houses developed systems on Windows NT to signal ease of maintenance and service availability, although conventional industry wisdom preferred UNIX-based systems. These processes have yet to be incorporated into diffusion models. In one of the first attempts, Moldovan, Goldenberg, and Chattopadhyay (2006) find that the perceived originality of the product influences the amount of word-of-mouth (and hence, the chances of adoption), and the perceived usefulness determines whether word-of-mouth will be positive or negative.

Another interesting research question addresses the question of how "seeding" (e.g., sampling and product demonstrations) stimulates the market's internal dynamics. A few works deal with the subject (Libai, Muller, and Peres 2005; Heiman and Muller 1996; Jain, Mahajan, and Muller 1995), but many issues are still unsolved.

The topic of diffusion through marketing channels is also under-researched. The use of marketing channels adds an additional layer of interdependencies to the diffusion process, since the actions and growth of channel members are linked together. Take, for example, a typical channel model as the one used by Jones and Ritz (1991), or Mesak and Darrat (2002) where the growth process is a double diffusion model: The product has to be diffused first among retailers and only then among the final consumers. On top of this model, additional interdependencies can be applied, for example, Lehmann and Weinberg (2000) introduce technological substitution into the distribution channel. They inspect the issue of sequential channels by examining the optimal timing of the video release of a movie. Usually video release pushes the movie sales down to zero; thus, there is a tradeoff between an early video release, which enhances video revenues, and a later video release, which is better for the movie revenues. Their empirical observation is that films are usually released to video later than optimal.

Research on diffusion and channels is in the incubation stage: A rich ground for research lies in combining topics in channel management and diffusion theory. Issues regarding vertical power distribution and issues from transaction cost analysis, such as concerning governance mechanism and their relative costs, have not yet been applied to growing markets; it is especially interesting to explore how channel management operations influence the communications flow and customer independencies in the market.

8
Diffusion and Social Networks

In traditional marketing, consumer interactions were regarded as an internal dynamic of the market that was beyond the direct influence of the firm. The importance of consumer interactions to the diffusion process—together with gradual decrease in the effectiveness of conventional advertising and the development of online social networks such as Facebook—have led firms to operate directly in the social networks of customers in their target markets, and invest marketing efforts in enhancing word-of-mouth among customers. In order to succeed in this daunting task, firms have to understand better how the structure and dynamics of the social network influence the diffusion process. In this chapter, we discuss new research on new product growth in social networks. We provide an overview of agent-based and network analysis, and discuss the dependency between the decision-making processes of individuals and the aggregate growth of the market.

The fundamental question in diffusion and social networks is how the social network structure influences growth. This question has not been yet answered theoretically, but was explored in some empirical studies (see Van den Bulte and Wuyts (2007) for an overview). Much of the research attention has been on the role of central individuals (influentials, social hubs) on the overall growth process (e.g., Goldenberg et al. 2009; Iyengar, Van den Bulte, and Valente 2008). Research into this question is still in its infancy, mainly due to the lack of data. New computational methods that enable large-scale sampling of online networks will probably boost further research.

From the modeling perspective, the basic question is how to incorporate the social network into the diffusion model. The implicit assumption of the Bass model and most of its extensions is that the social system is homogenous and fully connected and, thus, the adoption process can be represented by aggregate-level diffusion models. These models offer advantages and disadvantages: they are parsimonious and require little data for parameter estimation and forecasting; however, they provide little intuition as to how individual market interactions are linked to global market behavior (Parker 1994). Being focused on the aggregate number of adopters, they do not separate the effects of word-of-mouth, signals, and network externalities, which look similar at the aggregate level but represent totally different types of consumer interactions. Since the extensive recent research on social networks has revealed that they are neither homogenous nor fully connected (e.g., Kossinets and Watts 2006), and since consumer interactions other than word-of-mouth are becoming more important in today's innovations, aggregate-level modeling is no longer adequate. In order to deal with the complexity of interactions of heterogonous individuals in a partially connected network, the focus of diffusion modeling must shift to an individual-level perspective.

One well-known technique for describing a partially connected social network is via agent-based models, which describe the market as a collection of individual elements (termed *units*, *agents*, or *nodes*), interacting with each other through connections (termed *links*). The agents' behavior (in our case, adoption) is determined by a decision rule.

A typical agent-based model is the cellular automata of Goldenberg, Libai, and Muller (2001a) as illustrated in Figure 10. In their model each unit represents an individual consumer, and has a value of "0" if it has not yet adopted the product, and a value of "1" if it has adopted the product. Units adopt as a result of external influence (the parameter p) and internal influence (the parameter q). Time is discrete, and if in period t, an individual i is connected to $N_i(t)$ adopters, then the probability of adoption by that individual is shown by the following:

$$\text{Pr(adoption }|t)_i = 1 - (1 - p_i)(1 - q_i)^{N_i(t)} \tag{7}$$

Such a model overcomes some of the limitations of aggregate-level diffusion models. First, it enables researchers to distinguish between types of social influence; for example, Goldenberg, Libai, and Muller (2010) use it to explore network externalities by adding a threshold to the decision rule. It can be also used to separate the word-of-mouth ties from signals, by assigning different probabilities and dependencies on the righthand side of Equation 7. Second, this model allows heterogeneity by making p_i and q_i differ between units, or by setting different link structures to each unit. Heterogeneity can be incorporated into almost every aspect, including responsiveness to price and advertising (Libai, Muller, and Peres 2005), intrinsic innovativeness (Goldenberg, Libai, and Muller 2002), and role in the social network, that is, hubs, connectors, and experts (Goldenberg et al. 2009).

Another advantage of agent-based models is their ability to account for the spatial aspect of diffusion. Using a variation of cellular automata models called

Figure 10
Aggregate-level Decisions Generate the Cumulative Adoption Curve

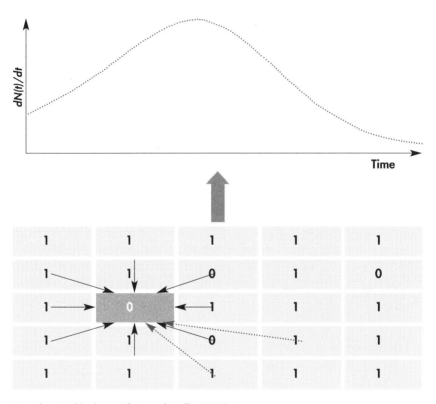

Based on Goldenberg, Libai, and Muller (2001a)

small world, Goldenberg, Libai, and Muller (2001b) study spatial issues in the market through the relative influence of strong and weak ties. They show that—consistent with Wuyts et al. (2004) and Rindfleisch and Moorman (2001)—the cumulative influence of weak ties has a strong effect on the growth process. Garber et al. (2004) suggest a measure of the spatial density of adoption in order to predict the product's success/failure.

Conceptually, aggregate diffusion models represent the overall results of individual-level processes. Therefore, in order to create a comprehensive and coherent market image, the individual-level and the aggregate-level formulations should be equivalent. However, the equivalence of these formulations is not straightforward. Previous studies have proposed methods of aggregating individual-level behavior based on assumptions regarding customer heterogeneity and calculation of the time to adoption (Van den Bulte and Stremersch 2004; Chatterjee and Eliashberg 1990). In the specific case of cellular automata, this equivalence is demonstrated by Goldenberg, Libai, and Muller (2001b), by relating the parameters p and q to the adoption hazard function, and presenting simulations that show that the individual level probability of adoption generates diffusion curves with p and q. The relationship between the Bass model and agent-based models is also investigated by Rahmandad and Streman (2008) and by Fibich, Gibori, and Muller (2009). Shaikh, Rangaswamy, and Balakrishnan (2006) show how the adoption of units in a small-world network can be aggregated to create the Bass model with some relatively simple assumptions. However, the interface between the individual level and aggregate level still does not have a closed formulation and needs to be further explored.

Although modeling of individual adoption decisions started in the 1970s (See Mahajan, Muller, and Bass (1990) for review), individual-level diffusion research is still in its early phases. Research so far has focused on developing the techniques and demonstrating them on sample problems; however, much more should be done to make individual-level models an integral part of the toolkit of diffusion research. As with any new, complex, and data-intensive method, these techniques must demonstrate that they can contribute insights that cannot be gained by the simple, parsimonious aggregate-level models.

9

New Product Growth in Specific Industries

Although diffusion models were originally designed to describe the diffusion of single-purchase durable goods, they have been extended to describe a wider variety of products and industries. In this chapter we review models that were customized from the Bass model to describe the market growth of new products in the entertainment, telecommunications, services, and pharmaceuticals industries.

Entertainment Products

Entertainment products—that is, films, books, and music—are sold in multi-billion dollars each year. According to Nielsen, the total box office revenues for films in the U.S. and Canada reached $9.78 billion, and book publishers' net revenues reached $37.26 billion in 2008. The fierce competition and the short life cycles of these products, together with their unique characteristics such as high seasonality, perishability, and distribution process, makes modeling their diffusion challenging yet highly important.

The penetration curve of many new entertainment products is different from the bell-shaped diffusion curve of Figure 4 (see page 16). In many cases, the curve for entertainment products is as presented in Figure 11—exponentially decreasing—where most of the sales are in their first week or two after launch. In order to fit such a pattern, the commonly used diffusion model for entertainment products (which was tested mainly on films) is of the following form (λ is a decay factor):

$$N(t) = m\,(1 - e^{-\lambda t}); \quad \frac{dN(t)}{dt} = \lambda e^{-\lambda t}. \tag{8}$$

This model is generated by the assumption that at every time interval Δt, a potential adopter makes a decision whether to adopt the product, with a probability $p = \lambda \Delta t$. The probability of the adoption decision occurring before time point t is $1 - (1-p)^N$, where $N = t/\Delta t$ is the number of trials between $[0,t]$. Taking

Δt to zero, the cumulative distribution function becomes $x(t) = 1 - e^{-\lambda t}$. The density function, that is, the probability that the adoption decision occurs in the interval $[t, t + \Delta t]$, is given by the derivative: $\lambda e^{-\lambda t}$. The expected cumulative number of adopters $N(t)$ at time t is $m \cdot x(t)$, (m is the market potential), which leads directly to Equation 8. Note that this model assumes that the adoption decisions do not depend on interactions by other customers; thus, consumer interactions are not included in this model. We address this issue below.

The exponentially decreasing pattern is not the only diffusion pattern in the industry. Using film penetration data, Sawhney and Eliashberg (1996) show that in additional to the films with exponentially decreasing sales (which they termed "blockbusters"), there are also "sleepers", whose sales function increases up to a maximum of three to six weeks after launch, and then decreases. To allow for this variance, they divide adoption into two periods, both after the launch: In the first period, the customer *decides* to see the movie; in the second period, the customer moves from decision to *action*, that is, actually sees the movie. Both processes are modeled using the above exponential function, where each time period has its own parameters.

Figure 11

Average Weekly Box Office Sales for the Film "Titanic"

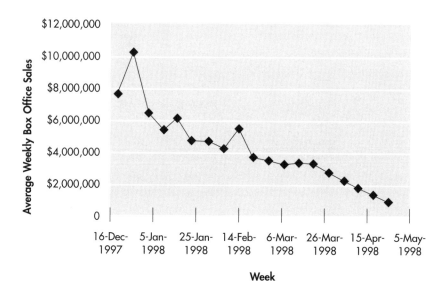

Table 8
Influence of Film Characteristic on Penetration

Characteristic	Influence
Genre (Drama)	Positive on the decay rate λ
Star power	Positive on the decay rate λ and the revenues
Mass advertising	Positive on the decay rate λ and the revenues
MPAA ratings	Negative influence on the market potential
Positive critics review	Positive on the revenues, although only in the long term
Number of screens	Mixed: Positive on the decay rate λ and the revenues
	A smaller effect under competition

The short life cycle of entertainment products has stimulated an interest in pre-launch forecasting. Eliashberg et al. (2000) propose a Markov individual-level model, where individuals switch between states (undecided, consideration, rejection, positive/negative word-of-mouth spreader, inactive), depending on both the film's and the customer's characteristics. The model is calibrated using a pre-release test group of viewers. Other pre-launch models have been proposed using previous penetration data (Lee, Boatwright, and Kamakura (2003) for music CDs), or advance purchase orders (Moe and Fader 2002).

Swami, Eliashberg, and Weinberg (1999) examine the planning problem of an exhibitor with multiple screens, who must decide which movies to screen and on which screens to present them. Lehmann and Weinberg (2000) also deal with planning issues resulting from the fast decay of the penetration curve, and investigate the optimal timing for issuing the video/DVD version of a movie. They conclude that currently movies are released to video later than optimal. Motivated by the need to provide forecasts with very small quantities of data, a group of studies investigates the movie and market factors influencing penetration (Ainslie, Drèze, and Zufryden 2005; Elberse and Eliashberg 2003; Zufryden 2000, 1996; Eliashberg and Shugan 1997). Their findings are summarized in Table 8.

The market for entertainment products is characterized by seasonal differences, with sales peaks during holiday seasons. High-season sales are responsible for 40%–90% of total annual sales (Radas and Shugan 1998). Radas and Shugan (1998) incorporate seasonality into the model by performing expansions and contractions on the time axis according to seasonal changes. During the high seasons, time flows faster, and the product passes more quickly through the stages in the life cycle.

Seasonality enhances competition in the market, since many products compete within a narrow time window. Competition has been shown to have a negative effect on revenues (Elberse and Eliashberg 2003) and decay rate (Ainslie, Drèze, and Zufryden 2005). Several studies deal with the issue of timing and planning competing entertainment products. Krider and Weinberg (1998) look for the optimal entry times that maximize the total revenues of two competing films, which differ in their initial appeal and their decay rates. Their results imply that the more appealing film should be released first. If both films have a slow decay rate, they can be released together. Ainslie, Drèze, and Zufryden (2005) add the influence of the film's characteristics to the appeal of the competing films by modeling the individual-level choice of a customer who chooses every week whether to go to a movie and which film to see.

As noted above, the commonly used model for penetration of entertainment products, in Equation 8 assumes that an individual adoption decision is independent of the adoption decisions of other individuals, namely, that there is no observable effect of consumer interactions. This assumption is not consistent with empirical findings that show strong internal market influences in entertainment markets (Eliashberg, Elberse, and Leenders 2006; Elberse and Eliashberg 2003; Eliashberg et al. 2000). One way to solve this inconsistency is by assuming "shadow diffusion". Generally, the term *shadow diffusion* relates to any diffusion processes that accompany the major diffusion process and influence it, yet are not captured in the standard adoption or sales data. Piracy is an example of shadow diffusion, and negative word-of-mouth might also be considered a form of shadow diffusion, as it is usually invisible to the firm (Goldenberg et al. 2007).

For entertainment markets, the shadow diffusion explanation suggests that the penetration process starts right when the pre-launch advertising launch starts. This advertising, together with consumer interactions, leads individuals to decide they want to adopt the product. However, their decision is not translated to actual purchase, since the product is not yet available. Therefore, this part of the process is hidden, or "shadowed". Only when the film is released, can customers realize their demand; thus, the penetration curve is "revealed." As illustrated in Figure 12, the shape of the revealed segment is determined by the time of release. For blockbusters, the launch appears after the peak of demand, and the observed curve is exponentially decreasing. For sleepers, on the other hand, fewer people have made early decisions; therefore the sales curve continues to increase also after launch, reaches the peak, and then decreases.

Figure 12
Blockbuster and Sleeper Movies with Hidden Pre-release Diffusion

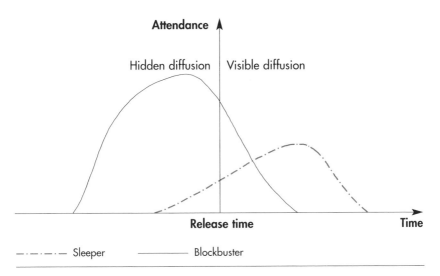

The advantage of a "shadow diffusion" model is that it is identical to the standard diffusion models used for other products, where the only difference is the fact that the product is not available at time zero. However, this approach has not yet been adopted by modelers of entertainment products. Although some studies refer to growth prior to launch, they do not use the standard diffusion model, but rather use models that do not include consumer interactions. Moe and Fader (2002), for example, explore advance purchase orders of music albums from CDNOW.com, using a Weibull distribution that does not offer a straightforward internal interaction parameter interpretation. Similarly, Hui, Eliashberg, and George (2008) construct a sophisticated optimal stopping rule in an individual-level behavioral model that captures the aggregate preorder and postrelease sales of motion picture DVDs, but they do not take consumer interactions into account in the individual decision making.

Telecommunications

Telecommunication products and services occupy an increasing share of the world's economies. According to the Telecommunications Industry Association, the global telecommunications industry revenue have reached $3.85 trillion in

2008 and the number of cellular subscribers around the world reached 4 billion at the end of 2008.

Fildes and Kumar (2002) list the characteristics of telecom markets that impose considerable challenge to diffusion research. Many telecom markets are growing markets; in addition, the penetration processes of telecom products are interrelated (e.g., penetration of unified messaging services depends on penetration of mobile phones) as well as dependent on the existence of infrastructures (e.g., Skype depends on broadband penetration). A single 3G telephony end-user application depends on hardware and software manufacturers, service providers, compatibility issues, and global infrastructures. Further, for some telecom products and services there are network externalities, and some services such as mobile services suffer from fierce competition and high churn rates. Chen and Watanabe (2006) explore a case study of information and communication technology in Japan, and show that the dynamic nature, competition, and technological substitution are high enough to overcome an embedded institutional rigidity so that the technology reached a deep penetration level.

Telecom markets form a rich substrate of research opportunities. They enable the investigation of interactions between market factors, and in most cases they are well documented and thus data are relatively easy to obtain. Many market processes in telecom are regulated, which in some scenarios keeps market variables under control and exposes hidden market mechanisms.

Despite this market richness, telecom products are mostly treated as if they were durable goods (Kauffman and Techatassanasoontron 2005; Botelho and Pinto 2004; Karine, Frank, and Laine 2004; Krishnan, Bass, and Kumar 2000; Jain, Mahajan, and Muller 1991). Some studies extend the Bass framework to seek methods for improving forecasting (Wareham, Levy, and Shi 2004; Islam, Feibig, and Meade 2002; Kumar, Nagpal, and Venkatesan 2002; Venkatesan and Kumar 2002). Kim, Mahajan, and Srivastava (1995) use the strong service orientation of information technology products to show a correlation between the market value of firms and the size of their customer base. Prins and Verhoef (2007) investigate the difference between the effects of individual and mass marketing communications on the adoption timing of a new telecommunication e-service among existing customers. They find both effects to be significant, yet differential, depending on the level of consumer loyalty. Due to the interesting pricing structure in mobile markets, some studies use their data to investigate pricing issues (Danaher, Hardie, and Putsis 2001, see Table 7). However, other issues treating the special dynamics of the telecom market have yet to be explored.

Services

Numerous new products introduced into the market during the last few decades are services. Such widely used services as cellular phones and multi-channel TV, and financial services such as direct banking, were not available before 1980. The growth of the Internet drove many new services offerings, among them instant messaging, shopping portals, online brokerage, and other services. Indeed, the service sector in the U.S. employs most of the work force, is responsible for more than 80% of the GDP, and is growing considerably faster than the goods sector (Zeithaml and Bitner 2003; BEA 2003).

The diffusion literature has generally modeled the diffusion of services as if they were durable goods, including categories such as cellular phones (Krishnan, Bass, and Kumar 2000), landline phones (Jain, Mahajan, and Muller 1991), cable TV (Lilien, Rangaswamy, and Van den Bulte 2000), and online banking (Hogan, Lemon, and Libai 2003). However, services differ from durable goods in several important aspects. First, many services involve multiple purchases, which might not directly affect the number of adopters, but will certainly influence the sales function. Recurrent purchase results in long-term relationships between customers and service providers; thus, relationship marketing becomes relevant to understanding the growth of services. In this regard, Yeon, Park, and Kim (2006) present a conceptual model that links satisfaction to adoption. They hypothesize (but do not show) that high satisfaction levels attract new customers, yet also increase the level of expectations, which in turn can lead to lower satisfaction and negatively influence word-of-mouth.

Gupta, Lehmann, and Stuart (2004) use the CRM concept of customer equity to show that in services, the value of the customer base can be an indicator of the market value of the firm. Using data on growth, profits, and retention rates of service firms such an Amazon, eBay, and Capital One, they calculate lifetime value and customer equity, and show a correlation to the stock exchange value of these firms.

An important aspect of services that can have considerable influence on the market growth of a new service is *customer attrition*. Libai, Muller, and Peres (2009b) compare the diffusion of services to filling a bucket with a hole: There is an inward flow of adopters, and a concurrent outward flow of departing customers. They suggest a model that incorporates attrition into the Bass diffusion model, at both the category and firm levels. Their category-level model assumes that some customers leave the new service, but eventually return because of service improvement, standards, lower prices, etc. Under this assumption, and if return probabilities are equal to those of initial adoption, then their model takes the following form:

$$\frac{dN(t)}{dt} = (p + \frac{qN(t)}{m}) \cdot (m - N(t)) - a\,N(t) \tag{9}$$

For a competitive market, the total attrition a has two components—one is the defection from the category, and the other is the churn between brands, denoted c; thus the model takes the form

$$\frac{dN_i(t)}{dt} = (p_i + \frac{q_i N_i(t)}{m}) \cdot (m - N(t)) - a_i\,N_i(t) + \sum_{j \neq i} \varepsilon_{ij}\,c_j\,N_j(t) \tag{10}$$

where the index i denotes the firm. The parameter ε_{ij} denotes the share of the churn of firm j that goes to firm i.

Neglecting attrition biases both parameter estimation and managerial diagnostics. In addition, attrition reduces the effective market potential of the service, and changes the time to maximum growth. Hogan, Lemon, and Libai (2003) investigate the loss due to defection of a customer in a growing market. Using market simulations, they show that the impact of a lost customer is especially high in the beginning of the life cycle when, due to the low number of customers, each customer has a larger relative interaction impact compared with that in later penetration stages.

Pharmaceuticals

As Stremersch notes in his introduction to the special issue on "Marketing and Health" of the *International Journal of Research in Marketing*: "Health and marketing is starting to gain firm ground as a new research field" (2009, page 229). Indeed, the interest among practitioners as well as academics in the marketing of health services and products has grown in the last 15 years as health care accounts for a growing percentage of GDP, reaching a level of 17% in the U.S. in 2008 (Keehan et al. 2008).

Some of this research used ethical or over-the-counter drugs as an example of the diffusion of new products. Thus, Desiraju, Nair, and Chintagunta 2004 (reviewed in the International Diffusion section) examine differences in diffusion parameters of drugs between countries. Hahn et al. (1994) focus on the repeat purchase of drugs, and built a two-stage model wherein consumers start at a trial stage (through a diffusion process), and then continue to repeat purchase (and also switch between brands) using a Markov process.

In developing new approaches and models, this new wave of research recognizes the unique nature of health care management and especially the idiosyncrasies of its supply chain management. Thus, Chintagunta and Desiraju (2005) examine the ROI of price promotions and detailing—which is a unique distribution method in pharmaceutical markets. However, as most of this research does not involve diffusion modeling or the growth of new pharmaceuticals, it will not be reviewed here. An exception is the dual market modeling by Vakratsas and Kolsarici (2008) that distinguishes between early market and main market adopters. Similar to saddle modeling (discussed on pages 24–26), their model distinguishes two segments by the tendency to adopt early or late, respectively. In the saddle literature the reasons for adopting early are not specified and in general are attributed to personal characteristics such as risk taking. In contrast, in the pharmaceutical case, early adopters are patients who have severe health problems and whose latent demand has accumulated prior to the drug's launch; the main market adopters are patients with milder conditions whose adoption may have been triggered by the launch itself. The result is a saddle, but unlike a traditional one, the adoption cycle begins with a high level of adoption and slowly declines, until it grows again due to new demand from the main market adopters.

An unexpected influence on the growth of pharmaceuticals in different countries is local regulation such as restrictions on physician prescription budgets and prohibition on direct-to-consumer advertising (DTCA). These restrictions tend to have differential effects for newly launched and mature drugs: budget restrictions hurt mature drugs more and DTCA prohibition has a larger effect on newly launched drugs (Stremersch and Lemmens 2009).

10
Choosing the Right Model

One of the challenges one has to face when implementing diffusion models is which model, of the large variety offered today, is the best to apply? Is an aggregate model more appropriate? Would an individual model provide more insights? Should one include international spillovers, competitive effects, or attrition? In this chapter we provide a decision flow chart to assist in the model choice for a particular managerial scenario in question (see Figure 13).

The guiding principle in this decision flow chart is to define the purpose of the analysis and the managerial scenarios, and match them to one of the available models. As an example, for a new durable good operating in a strong competitive market, where all competing brands approach the same target markets, the appropriate diffusion model would be Equation 4.

Note that this flow chart is far from complete—most models extend to the basic diffusion scenario only in a single dimension. Thus, if the managerial scenario is complex (e.g., involves competition, technology generations, and marketing models), no available model can fully describe it, and the chosen model should be the one which describes more closely the important dimensions.

Aggregate versus Individual

Figure 13 describes aggregate-level models. Given the increased use of individual-level models and the availability of large-scale individual-level data and the powerful insights they provide, one might ask whether an individual-level model (such as those described in Chapter 8) should be chosen rather than the aggregate-level model.

Implementing individual-level models requires technical sophistication and programming skills (see www.complexmarkets.com for Excel-based implementation). Their usage is especially worthwhile if the marketing scenario in question satisfies the following criteria:

High level of heterogeneity in the population The population is heterogenic in aspects that are relevant to adoption diffusion (Libai, Muller, and Peres 2005), and there is information as to the distribution of this heterogeneity.

Figure 13
Flowchart for Choosing an Aggregate Diffusion Model

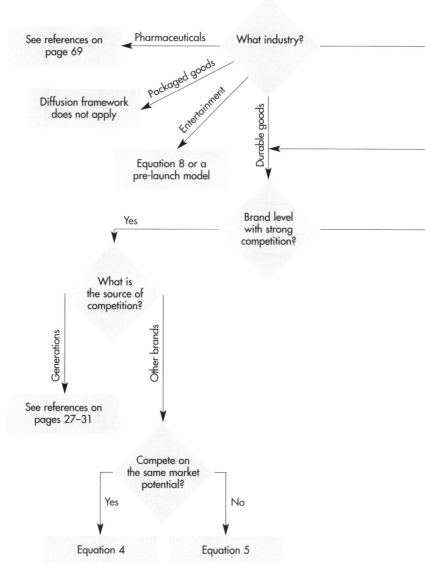

Start here

See references on
page 69
← Pharmaceuticals ← What industry?

Packaged goods

Diffusion framework
does not apply

Entertainment

Durable goods

Equation 8 or a
pre-launch model

Yes

Brand level
with strong
competition?

What is
the source of
competition?

Generations

Other brands

See references on
pages 27–31

Compete on
the same market
potential?

Yes   No

Equation 4   Equation 5

* If strong non-exponential effects of marketing mix are present, modify the chosen model to a Generalized Bass form
(Equation 6).
* In case of little or no data, use analogies as explained on page 17.

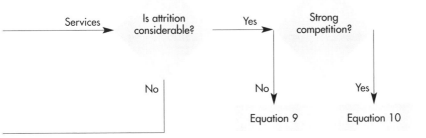

Services → Is attrition considerable? —Yes→ Strong competition?

No | No ↓ Yes ↓

Equation 9   Equation 10

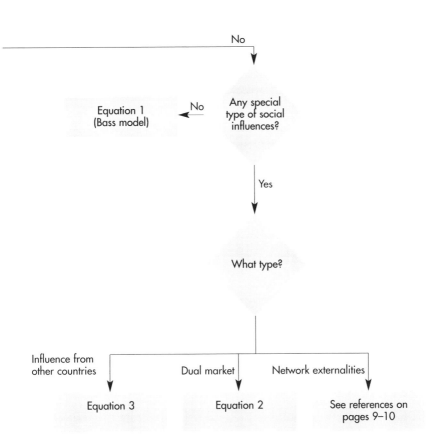

No ↓

Equation 1
(Bass model) ←No— Any special type of social influences?

Yes ↓

What type?

Influence from other countries   Dual market   Network externalities

Equation 3   Equation 2   See references on pages 9–10

Network structure is important The network is not fully connected and the connectivity structure is important to the growth process; the interplay of weak ties and strong ties matters (Goldenberg, Libai, and Muller 2001a); or there are questions regarding spatial effects (Garber et al. 2004).

High level of randomness Randomness in the social system is high, especially if it is asymmetric and biased towards a specific direction.

Complex adoption decision The adoption decision, or the nature of communications, is complex, involving negative word-of-mouth (Goldenberg et al. 2007), time delays, topic choice (Stephen and Berger 2009), multiple-stage decisions, etc.

11
Knowledge Gaps in Innovation Diffusion

Five decades of research in diffusion have contributed greatly to our understanding of the evolution of innovation markets. Research is constantly moving beyond the basic diffusion scenario of a monopoly of durable goods, toward exploring a variety of scenarios and customer interactions. We can describe with greater accuracy turning points in the product life cycle, including take-offs, saddles, and technological substitution. We have a better knowledge of the effect of competition, advertising, pricing, and cross-country influences on growth. We have begun exploring how the structure of the social network influences the contagion process. The focus given to specific industries, such as entertainment, telecommunication, services, and pharmaceuticals, has revealed their idiosyncrasies and provided managers with better tools to manage their diffusion processes.

Despite this progress, we still lack information on some important aspects of diffusion. We describe below four areas in need of research attention.

From Individual Decision Making to Market Growth

The market evolution of a new product is the aggregate outcome of the adoption decisions of many individuals. Since marketing tools such as advertising, price, exposure, and loyalty programs operate at the individual level, but growth and profits outcomes are aggregate, connecting individual adoption to aggregate outcomes is highly important to practitioners in growing markets.

Although researchers began modeling individual adoption decisions in the 1970s (see Mahajan, Muller, and Bass 1990 for review), we still know little about how adoption decisions are made, and how these individual decisions combine to an overall diffusion pattern. Specifically, there are four major knowledge gaps:

The Roles of Social Influences The three main types of social influences—word-of-mouth, signals, and network externalities—are all embedded in the parameter q in the Bass model. Some research attempted to disentangle these influences, such as the works reviewed here on network externalities, but more knowledge is needed in order for managers to exercise some control over these influences. For example, different types of word-of-mouth (e.g., within- and cross-brand, positive versus negative) should be investigated; models should separate various signals from word-of-mouth (e.g., weak ties vs. cross-country signals, or cross-brand influences), and the signaling effect of marketing mix variables should be studied. In addition, more empirical studies are needed to find ways to identify, isolate, and measure the three types of influences, their antecedents, and their influence on market growth.

The Influence of Social Network Structure on Growth The basic diffusion models assume fully connected networks; however, actual social networks are far from being fully connected, and most individuals are engaged in a limited number of connections (Watts and Dodds 2007). A few studies focus on breaks in connectivity and their implications (Goldenberg, Libai, and Muller 2001a, 2002), yet much needs to be done. Specifically, empirical findings on partial connectivity structures and the role of adopter groups such as experts, mavens, and opinion leaders in diffusion (e.g., Goldenberg et al. 2009), should be integrated into such models.

The online medium opens the opportunity to obtain individual-level data, yet it introduces entirely new types of influence: blogs, sites like LinkedIn, and message boards like Yahoo!Finance make it perfectly plausible that strangers might have greater influence than family and friends in adoption of many product categories. We need a better understanding of the relative influence of these types of online tools in order for marketers to influence the nature of the diffusion process. We do not fully understand the sources of influence at different stages of the online adoption process, for example, awareness via search engines, consideration via online shops, and purchase in retail outlets. In the physical world, awareness, consideration, choice, and purchase often occur together, but in online markets, influence can occur in one medium, and transaction can occur in another.

The Role of Consumer Heterogeneity As discussed in Chapter 2, an alternative approach to social contagion suggests that diffusion is a result of heterogeneity in various aspects (innovativeness, price, function) in the adopting population. While it is clear that populations are heterogeneous, and that both heterogeneity and social contagion exist in social systems, it is still unclear which market behaviors are dominated by social processes, which are outcomes of heterogeneity among adopters, and which are a mixture of both. Understanding heterogeneity is going to be ever more urgent as markets become more heterogeneous, products are launched globally, developing countries are engaged in diffusion processes, and adopters are influenced through blogs and user forums by people who might be very different from them.

This important and yet under-researched area can be investigated in two ways: modeling and empirical studies. Individual-level diffusion models can be effective tools to test the aggregate outcomes of heterogeneity. Empirical studies can develop proxies for the two phenomena and compare the results of diffusion studies across cultures to disentangle the effects. Van den Bulte and Stremersch (2004) and Van den Bulte and Lilien (2001) are examples of empirical analyses that shed light on the balance between heterogeneity and social contagion.

Adoption Decisions and the Hierarchy of Effects Existing research does not provide a good answer as to how adoption decisions go through the hierarchy of effects (awareness, consideration, liking, choice, and purchase). Does the adoption decision occur at the purchase stage or earlier? What is the time dynamic of going through the hierarchy? How does this hierarchy influence, and how is this hierarchy influenced by communications between individuals in various stages? Answering these questions is essential for better diagnostics and forecasting, as well as for the application of the proper managerial tools in each stage.

Diffusion in the Developing World

Developing countries form highly growing potential markets for innovations. The World Bank Report for 2008 indicates that while GDP annual growth rates in developed countries are expected to remain around 2% for the coming years, developing countries are forecasted to continue their stable and consistent growth of over 7% per year (The World Bank Report 2008).

Diffusion of innovations in developing countries has unique patterns, which are rarely found in developed countries. For example, in the mobile industry, the standard consumption pattern in developed countries is of one user per handset; however, in many developing countries, one mobile handset can serve several family members, each with his or her private SIM card. Sometimes handsets can accept only incoming calls or call only certain numbers (Chircu and Mahajan 2009). While handsets are frequently updated in developed countries, in developing regions there is an active market for secondhand handsets (Mahajan 2009).

Current demographic changes raise new challenges for global marketers. With large immigration waves, many families—representing strongly tied units in the social network—are dispersed between remote geographic locales, challenging the traditional association of strong ties with geographical proximity. This dispersion influences both launch policy (for example, should Bollywood films be launched simultaneously in India and outside India?) and product design and offering (for example, should a cellular price deal include long-distance air time that enables calling relatives overseas?).

Although developing countries usually fall behind developed countries in the propensity to adopt innovations (The World Bank Report 2008, pg. 5), they are highly responsive to specific innovations that answer their special needs (Chircu and Mahajan 2009). As an example, executives of Comverse Technology recall that the early adopters for an innovative product in the mid-1990s—voice mail—were telephone service providers from Africa and India, whose subscribers used public phones and needed a private voice mail box. The usage of one handset by multiple users boosted the penetration of prepaid cards in developing countries, and motivated service providers to come up with creative mechanisms of separating billing for a single handset (Mahajan 2009). In another example, customers in developing countries save airtime by using ringtones to transfer messages, so they use ringtones and ringtone control functions much more intensively than the average user in developed countries.

Despite the richness of these phenomena and the growing availability of data, the unique diffusion patterns in developing countries are still collected as anecdotal evidence, and are not incorporated into diffusion models. With the exception of a few papers (e.g., Desiraju, Nair, and Chintagunta 2004), research has not explored whether such patterns are country specific or abundant across emerging economies, whether they are generated by growth drivers similar to those for developed countries, and what actions firms might take in order to maximize their profits under such growth patterns.

Diffusion at the Brand Level

As competitive structures become more complex, brand-level decision making takes on crucial importance to understanding growth. As discussed in Chapter 6, the underlying assumption in most competitive diffusion studies is that brand- and category-level decision making is similar; however, further research is needed to check whether this assumption is realistic. Our knowledge is lacking in three main areas:

The Brand Choice Process If brand choice is a two-stage process, wherein consumer interactions are dominant in category choice, and special offers and advertising are dominant in choosing the brand, the straightforward application of a standard diffusion model on brand-level data is problematic. Turning points, such as takeoff, saddles, and peaks at the brand level, have a different meaning from those at the category level and might be driven by different processes (Libai, Muller, and Peres 2009a). Behavioral studies and diffusion models that combine choice and individual-level decision processes to better understand the brand choice process and its influence on the overall growth.

Market Potential Do competing brands draw from one market potential, or does each brand have its own market potential? While we believe the former, models of both scenarios should be empirically compared on a large set of data to resolve this issue.

Influence of Competition along the Distribution Chain Basic diffusion models should be extended to be both multi-layer and competitive. For example, in the mobile phone industry, while competing operators distribute the same handset model, third parties offer customers auto-selection of the network with the best rate. Besides the complex cross-firm dynamics, such scenarios bear implications for the customers' brand perception in such an environment, and in turn the brand strategy that will optimize growth.

The Influence of Product Characteristics and the Distribution Chain

Of the four Ps of the marketing mix, diffusion research has thus far generated a large body of knowledge concerning the effects of price and promotion, yet little has been done concerning the other two elements: product and place.

Product Although popular literature discusses the way a new product should be designed in order to diffuse better than other products (Heath and Heath 2007), research literature provides little insight into this question. The massive research in choice modeling deals with the match between product attributes and preferences, but the communication aspect, which is so important in diffusion, is missing. Additional product-related modeling questions should address interdependencies between products. For instance, with Amazon.com offering more than 250,000 music albums as well as various book formats, portfolio decisions become crucial to a new product's success. Allocation of marketing efforts, such as whether to focus on a limited number of blockbusters or spread efforts over many long-tailed products (Elberse 2008), are of great managerial interest. Extending the basic diffusion model to include multi-product interactions can contribute to the discussion.

Place In addition to traditional distribution systems, novel distribution mechanisms are emerging, some with a complex distribution structure such as service providers and retailers that both distribute mobile handsets, and others representing direct consumer involvement such as eBay and Netflix. Diffusion modeling should aim to explore the influence of these novel distribution structures on growth, as well as answer normative questions such as the optimal distribution chain under various types of social networks, and extent of firm support of user-involved channels.

Technical Appendix: Hazard Modeling

The proportional hazard model is the primary tool that researchers use to model turning points in the product lifecycle. We begin with a somewhat different interpretation of the Bass model and then describe the hazard model. An elegant and exhaustive treatment of the subject, including estimation issues, can be found in Bass, Jain, and Krishnan (2000).

Let $f(t)$ and $F(t)$ be the current percentage of adoption out of a fixed market potential, and the cumulative percentage, respectively. The Bass model can be written as

$$f(t)/(1 - F(t)) = p + qF(t) \qquad\qquad (A1)$$

The parameters p and q are the external and internal influence coefficients. In Bass' 1969 paper, as well as later interpretations that regarded diffusion as a theory of interpersonal communications, the parameter p represented advertising, and q represented word-of-mouth communications. More recently, the internal coefficient q is interpreted as the parameter that represents *consumer interdependencies* in all its manifestations: signals, externalities, and interpersonal communications. Thus, more recent models must take into account the idiosyncratic effects of these consumers' interdependencies.

The lefthand side of Equation A1 is the hazard rate, namely, the conditional probability that a person will adopt (in the next instant of time) given that he or she has not adopted up to time t. Thus, this interpretation of the Bass model implies that the hazard rate of adoption—the probability of adoption at time t conditional on not adopting before that time—is a linear function of the adopting population. The Generalized Bass model (Bass, Krishnan, and Jain 1994) is given by

$$f(t)/(1 - F(t)) = (p + qF(t)) \cdot \phi\,(z(t)) \qquad\qquad (A2)$$

The vector $z(t)$ is an array of marketing variables such as advertising and price, and ϕ is some continuous function. In Bass, Krishnan, and Jain (1994), the variables appeared in percent change and the function ϕ was set to be linear.

The proportional hazard model begins with an event occurring at time t—a random variable with a density function $f(t)$ and distribution function $F(t)$. In the takeoff literature branch, the event is a takeoff; in the diffusion stream the event is the time to adoption. In order to see the relationship between the hazard model approach and the classical Bass model, assume the latter event, i.e., t, is the time to adoption.

Let $h(t, z(t))$ be the hazard rate of adoption for an individual, i.e., the conditional probability that an individual will adopt the product at time t, given that he or she has not adopted prior to this time, and that the set of marketing variables at time t is given by $z(t)$. Clearly,

$$h(t, z) = f(t)/(1 - F(t)) \tag{A3}$$

The Cox hazard rate can be written as:

$$h(t, z(t)) = h_0(t)\, \phi\, (z\, (t)) \tag{A4}$$

$h_0(t)$ is the baseline hazard function, and $\phi\, (z\, (t))$ is a continuous function of the marketing variables that is usually assumed to be exponential.

The relationship to the Generalized Bass model is achieved by further assuming that the baseline hazard function is a linear function of F, i.e., $h_0(t) = p + qF(t)$. Substituting this and Equation A3 into Equation A4 yields the same function as the Generalized Bass model:

$$f(t)/(1 - F(t)) = (p + qF(t)) \cdot \phi\, (z\, (t)) \tag{A5}$$

If the market potential is m, then multiplication of Equation A5 and Equation A2 by m yields the same equation with the same interpretation (with $N(t) = mF(t)$, and thus $\dfrac{dN(t)}{dt} = mF(t)$):

$$\frac{dN(t)}{dt} = (p + \frac{qN(t)}{m}) \cdot (m - N(t)) \cdot \phi\, (z\, (t)) \tag{A6}$$

One should note that though the equations are identical, the estimation procedures of the Bass (or Generalized Bass) and the proportional hazard model are usually different. Bass, Jain, and Krishnan (2000) report the result of the estimation procedures for three consumer durables where in two out of the three cases the proportional hazard model did better than the Generalized Bass model, albeit with rather minute improvement.

Although the proportional hazard model can be used to estimate the effects of marketing variables in growth as in Bass, Jain, and Krishnan (2000), it can also be used for estimating the occurrence of a specific turning point in the product life cycle, such as takeoff (Golder and Tellis 1997), duration of the growth stage (Stremersch and Tellis 2004), saddle (Van den Bulte and Joshi 2007), and technological substitution (Danaher, Hardie, and Putsis 2001).

References

Agarwal, Rajshree, and Barry L. Bayus (2002), "The Market Evolution and Takeoff of Product Innovations." *Management Science* 48 (8), 1024–41.

Ainslie, Andrew, Xavier Drèze, and Fred S. Zufryden (2005), "Modeling Movie Life Cycles and Market Share." *Marketing Science* 24 (3), 508–17.

Allaway, Arthur W., William C. Black, Michael D. Richard, and Barry J. Mason (1994), "Evolution of a Retail Market Area: An Event-History Model of Spatial Diffusion." *Economic Geography* 70 (1), 23–40.

Bailey, Norman T.J. (1957), *The Mathematical Theory of Epidemics*. London, U.K.: Charles Griffin and Co.

Bass, Frank M. (1969), "A New Product Growth Model for Consumer Durables." *Management Science* 15 (5), 215–27.

Bass, Frank M. (1980), "The Relationship Between Diffusion Rates, Experience Curves, and Demand Elasticities for Consumer Durable Technological Innovations." *Journal of Business* 53 (3), 51–67.

Bass, Frank M., Dipak C. Jain, and Trichy V. Krishnan (2000), "Modeling the Marketing-Mix in New-Product Diffusion." In *New-Product Diffusion Models*, eds. Vijay Mahajan, Eitan Muller, and Yoram Wind, Chapter 5, 99–122. New York, N.Y.: Kluwer Academic Publisher.

Bass, Frank M., Trichy V. Krishnan, and Dipak C. Jain (1994), "Why the Bass Model Fits Without Decision Variables." *Marketing Science* 13 (3), 203–23.

Bass, Portia, and Frank M. Bass (2001), "Diffusion of Technology Generations: A Model of Adoption and Repeat Sales." Dallas, Tex.: University of Texas at Dallas, Working Paper.

Bass, Portia, and Frank M. Bass (2004), "IT Waves: Two Completed Generational Diffusion Models." Dallas, Tex.: University of Texas at Dallas, Working Paper.

Bayus, Barry L. (1992), "Dynamic Pricing of Next-Generation Consumer Durables." *Marketing Science* 11 (3), 251–65.

Bayus, Barry L. (1994), "Are Product Life Cycles Really Getting Shorter?" *Journal of Product Innovation Management* 11 (4), 300–8.

Bayus, Barry L. (1998), "An Analysis of Product Lifetimes in a Technologically Dynamic Industry." *Management Science* 44 (6), 763–75.

BEA (2003), Bureau of Economic Analysis, US Department of Commerce, GDP by Industry, http://www.bea.gov/bea/pn/GDPbyInd_GO_NAICS.xls.

Berger, Jonah, and Chip Heath (2007), "When Consumers Diverge from Others: Identity Signaling and Product Domains." *Journal of Consumer Research* 34 (2), 121–34.

Berger, Jonah, and Chip Heath (2008), "Who Drives Divergence? Identity Signaling, Out-Group Similarity, and the Abandonment of Cultural Tastes." *Journal of Personality and Social Psychology* 95 (3) 593–607.

Binken, Jeroen L.G., and Stefan Stremersch (2009), "The Effect of Superstar Software on Hardware Sales in System Markets." *Journal of Marketing* 73 (2), 88–104.

Boswijk, Peter H., and Philip Hans Franses (2005), "On the Econometrics of the Bass Diffusion Model." *Journal of Business & Economic Statistics* 23 (3), 255–88.

Botelho, Anabela, and Ligia Costa Pinto (2004), "The Diffusion of Cellular Phones in Portugal." *Telecommunications Policy* 28 (5–6), 427–37.

Bottomley, Paul A., and Robert Fildes (1998), "The Role of Prices in Models of Innovation Diffusion." *Journal of Forecasting* 17 (7), 539–55.

Bourdieu, Pierre (1984), *Distinction: A Social Critique of the Judgment of Taste.* Cambridge, Mass.: Harvard University Press.

Bronnenberg, Bart J., and Vijay Mahajan (2001), "Unobserved Retail Behavior in Multimarket Data: Joint Spatial Dependence in Market Shares and Promotional Variables." *Marketing Science* 20 (3), 284–99.

Bronnenberg, Bart J., Vijay Mahajan, and Wilfried R. Vanhonacker (2000), "The Emergence of Market Structure in New Repeat-Purchase Categories: The Interplay of Market Share and Retail Distribution." *Journal of Marketing Research* 37 (1), 16–31.

Bronnenberg, Bart J., and Carl F. Mela (2004), "Market Roll–Out and Retailer Adoption for New Brands." *Marketing Science* 23 (4), 500–18.

Burt, Ronald S. (1987), "Social Contagion and Innovation: Cohesion versus Structural Equivalence." *American Journal of Sociology* 92 (6), 1287–335.

Chandrasekaran, Deepa, and Gerard J. Tellis (2007), "A Critical Review of Marketing Research on Diffusion of New Products." In *Review of Marketing Research* (vol. 3), ed. Naresh K. Malhotra, Chapter 2, 39–80. Armonk, N.Y.: M.E. Sharpe, Inc.

Chandrasekaran, Deepa, and Gerard J. Tellis (2008), "Global Takeoff of New Products: Culture, Wealth, or Vanishing Differences?" *Marketing Science* 27 (5), 844–60.

Chatterjee, Rabikar, and Jehoshua Eliashberg (1990), "The Innovation Diffusion Process in a Heterogeneous Population: A Micromodeling Approach." *Management Science* 36 (9), 1057–79.

Chatterjee, Rabikar, Jehoshua Eliashberg, and Vithala R. Rao (2000), "Dynamic Models Incorporating Competition." In *New-Product Diffusion Models*, eds. Vijay Mahajan, Eitan Muller, and Yoram Wind, Chapter 8, 165–206. New York, N.Y.: Kluwer Academic Publisher.

Chen, Chaojung, and Chihiro Watanabe (2006), "Diffusion, Substitution and Competition Dynamism inside the ICT Market: The Case of Japan." *Technological Forecasting and Social Change* 73 (6), 731–58.

Chintagunta, Pradeep K., and Ramarao Desiraju (2005), "Strategic Pricing and Detailing Behavior in International Markets." *Marketing Science* 24 (1), 67–80.

Chircu, Alina M., and Vijay Mahajan (2009), "Revisiting Digital Divide: An Analysis of Mobile Technology Depth and Service Breadth in the BRIC Countries." *Journal of Product Innovation Management* 26 (4), 455–66.

Danaher, Peter J., Bruce G. S. Hardie, and William P. Putsis (2001), "Marketing-mix Variables and the Diffusion of Successive Generations of Technological Innovation." *International Journal of Marketing Research* 38 (4), 501–14.

De Bruyn, Arnaud, and Gary Lilien (2008), "A Multi-Stage Model of Word-of-mouth Influence Through Viral Marketing." *International Journal of Research in Marketing* 25 (3), 151–63.

Debruyne, Marion, and David J. Reibstein (2005), "Competitor See, Competitor Do: Incumbent Entry in New Market Niches." *Marketing Science* 24 (1), 55–66.

Dekimpe, Marnik G., Philip M. Parker, and Miklos Sarvary (1998), "Staged Estimation of International Diffusion Models: An Application to Global Cellular Telephone Adoption." *Technological Forecasting and Social Change* 57(1), 105–32.

Dekimpe, Marnik G., Philip M. Parker, and Miklos Sarvary (2000a), "Multimarket and Global Diffusion." In *New-Product Diffusion Models*, eds. Vijay Mahajan, Eitan Muller, and Yoram Wind, Chapter 3, 49–73. New York, N.Y.: Kluwer Academic Publisher.

Dekimpe, Marnik G., Philip M. Parker, and Miklos Sarvary (2000b), "Global Diffusion of Technological Innovations: A Coupled-Hazard Approach." *Journal of Marketing Research* 37 (1), 47–59.

Dekimpe, Marnik G., Philip M. Parker, and Miklos Sarvary (2000c), "Globalization: Modeling Technology Adoption Timing across Countries." *Technological Forecasting and Social Change* 63 (1), 25–42.

Desiraju, Ramarao, Harikesh Nair, and Pradeep Chintagunta (2004), "Diffusion of New Pharmaceutical Drugs in Developing and Developed Nations." *International Journal of Research in Marketing* 21 (4), 341–57.

Dwyer, Sean, Hani Mesak, and Maxwell Hsu (2005), "An Exploratory Examination of the Influence of National Culture on Cross-National Product Diffusion." *Journal of International Marketing* 13 (2), 1–27.

Eaton, Jonathan, and Samuel Kortum (1999), "International Technology Diffusion: Theory and Measurement." *International Economic Review* 40 (3), 537–70.

Elberse, Anita (2008), "Should You Invest in the Long Tail?" *Harvard Business Review* (July–August), 1–10.

Elberse, Anita, and Jehoshua Eliashberg (2003), "Demand and Supply Dynamics for Sequentially Released Products in International Markets: The Case of Motion Pictures." *Marketing Science* 22 (3), 329–54.

Eliashberg, Jehoshua, Anita Elberse, and Mark Leenders (2006), "The Motion Picture Industry: Critical Issues in Practice, Current Research, and New Research Directions." *Marketing Science* 25 (6), 638–61.

Eliashberg, Jehoshua, and Kristiaan Helsen (1996), "Modeling Lead/Lag Phenomena in Global Marketing: The Case of VCRs." Philadelphia, Penn.: University of Pennsylvania, Working Paper.

Eliashberg, Jehoshua, Jedid-Jah Jonker, Mohanbir S. Sawhney, and Berend Wierenga (2000), "Moviemod: An Implementable Decision Support System for Pre-Release Market Evaluation of Motion Pictures." *Marketing Science* 19 (3), 226–43.

Eliashberg, Jehoshua, and Steven M. Shugan (1997), "Film Critics: Influencers or Predictors?" *Journal of Marketing* 61 (2), 68–78.

Fader, Peter H. and Bruce G.S. Hardie (2001), "Forecasting Repeat Sales at CDNOW: A Case Study." *Interfaces* 31 (3), S94–107.

Feichtinger, Gustav (1992), "Hopf Bifurcation in an Advertising Diffusion Model." *Journal of Economic Behavior and Organization* 17 (3), 401–11.

Fibich, Gadi, Ro'i Gibori, and Eitan Muller (2009), "Analysis of Cellular Automata Diffusion Models in Marketing." Tel Aviv, Israel: Tel Aviv University, Working Paper.

Fildes, Robert, and V. Kumar (2002), "Telecommunications Demand Forecasting–A Review." *International Journal of Forecasting* 18 (4), 489–522.

Foster, Joseph A., Peter N. Golder, and Gerard J. Tellis (2004), "Predicting Sales Takeoff for Whirlpool's New Personal Valet." *Marketing Science* 23 (2), 182–5.

Ganesh, Jaishankar (1998), "Converging Trends Within The European Union: Insights from an Analysis of Diffusion Patterns." *Journal of International Marketing* 6 (4), 32–48.

Ganesh, Jaishankar, and V. Kumar (1996), "Capturing the Cross-national Learning Effect: An Analysis of Industrial Technology Diffusion." *Journal of the Academy of Marketing Science* 24 (4), 328–37.

Ganesh, Jaishankar, V. Kumar, and Velavan Subramaniam (1997), "Learning Effect in Multinational Diffusion of Consumer Durables: An Exploratory Investigation." *Journal of the Academy of Marketing Science* 25 (3), 214–28.

Garber, Tal, Jacob Goldenberg, Barak Libai, and Eitan Muller (2004), "From Density to Destiny: Using Spatial Dimension of Sales Data for Early Prediction of New Product Success." *Marketing Science* 23 (3), 419–28.

Giraldo, Ospina J., and Hincapie D. Palacio (2008), "Deterministic SIR (Susceptible-Infected-Removed) Models Applied to Varicella Outbreaks." *Epidemiology and Infection* 136 (5), 679–87.

Givon, Moshe, Vijay Mahajan, and Eitan Muller (1995), "Software Piracy: Estimation of Lost Sales and the Impact on Software Diffusion." *Journal of Marketing* 59 (1), 29–37.

Givon, Moshe, Vijay Mahajan, and Eitan Muller (1997), "Assessing the Relationship Between the User-Based Market Share and Unit Sales-Based Market Share for Pirated Software Brands in Competitive Markets." *Technological Forecasting and Social Change* 55 (2), 131–44.

Godes, David, and Dina Mayzlin (2009), "Firm-Created Word-of-Mouth Communication: Evidence from a Field Study." *Marketing Science* 28 (4), 721–39.

Goldenberg, Jacob, Sangman Han, Donald R. Lehmann, and Jae Weon Hong (2009), "The Role of Hubs in Adoption Processes." *Journal of Marketing* 73 (2), 1–13.

Goldenberg, Jacob, Barak Libai, and Eitan Muller (2001a), "Using Complex Systems Analysis to Advance Marketing Theory Development: Modeling Heterogeneity Effects on New Product Growth Through Stochastic Cellular Automata." *Academy of Marketing Science Review* [online] 2001(9).

Goldenberg, Jacob, Barak Libai, and Eitan Muller (2001b), "Talk of the Network: A Complex System Look at the Underlying Process of Word of Mouth." *Marketing Letters* 12 (3), 211–23.

Goldenberg, Jacob, Barak Libai, and Eitan Muller (2002), "Riding the Saddle: How Cross-Market Communications Can Create a Major Slump In Sales." *Journal of Marketing* 66 (2), 1–16.

Goldenberg, Jacob, Barak Libai, and Eitan Muller (2010), "The Chilling Effect of Network Externalities." *International Journal of Research in Marketing*, forthcoming.

Goldenberg, Jacob, Barak Libai, Eitan Muller, and Sarit Moldovan (2007), "The NPV of Bad News." *International Journal of Research in Marketing* 24 (3), 186–200.

Goldenberg, Jacob, and Shaul Oreg (2007), "Laggards in Disguise: Resistance to Adopt and the Leapfrogging Effect." *Technological Forecasting and Social Change* 74 (8), 1272–81.

Golder, Peter N. (1994), "Beyond Diffusion: An Explanatory Model of Takeoff and Growth Sales for Consumer Durables." Los Angeles, Calif.: University of Southern California, Los Angeles, Unpublished Ph.D. dissertation.

Golder, Peter N., and Gerard J. Tellis (1997), "Will It Ever Fly? Modeling the Takeoff of Really New Consumer Durables." *Marketing Science* 16 (3), 256–70.

Golder, Peter N., and Gerard J. Tellis (1998), "Beyond Diffusion: An Affordability Model of the Growth of New Consumer Durables." *Journal of Forecasting* 17 (3–4), 259–80.

Golder, Peter N., and Gerard J. Tellis (2004), "Growing, Growing, Gone: Cascades, Diffusion, and Turning Points in the Product Life Cycle." *Marketing Science* 23 (2), 207–28.

Granovetter, Mark (1978), "Threshold Models of Collective Behavior." *American Journal of Sociology* 83 (May), 1420–43.

Gupta, Sunil, Donald R. Lehmann, and Jennifer Ames Stuart (2004), "Valuing Customers." *Journal of Marketing Research* 41 (1), 7–18.

Hahn, Minhi, Sehoon Park, Lakshman Krishnamurti, and Andris A. Zoltners (1994), "Analysis of New Product Diffusion Using a Four-Segment Trial-Repeat Model." *Marketing Science* 13 (3), 224–47.

Haruvy, Ernan, Vijay Mahajan, and Ashutosh Prasad (2004), "The Effect of Piracy on the Market Penetration of Subscription Software." *Journal of Business* 77 (2), S81–108.

Hauser, John, Gerard J. Tellis, and Abbie Griffin (2006), "Research on Innovation: A Review and Agenda for Marketing Science." *Marketing Science* 25 (6), 687–717.

Heath, Chip, and Dan Heath (2007), *Made to Stick: Why Some Ideas Survive and Others Die*. New York, N.Y.: Random House.

Heiman, Amir, and Eitan Muller (1996), "Using Demonstration to Increase New Product Acceptance: Controlling Demonstration Time." *Journal of Marketing Research* 33 (4), 1–11.

Helsen, Kristiaan, Kamel Jedidi, and Wayne S. DeSarbo (1993), "A New Approach to Country Segmentation Utilizing Multinational Diffusion Patterns." *Journal of Marketing* 57 (4), 60–71.

Henard, David H., and David M. Szymanski (2001), "Why Some New Products Are More Successful Than Others." *Journal of Marketing Research* 28 (3), 362–75.

Ho, Teck-Hua, Sergei Savin, and Christian Terwiesch (2002), "Managing Demand and Sales Dynamics in New Product Diffusion under Supply Constraint." *Management Science* 48 (2), 187–206.

Hofstede, Geert (2001), *Culture's Consequences*. Thousand Oaks, Calif.: Sage Publications.

Hogan, John E., Katherine N. Lemon, and Barak Libai (2003), "What Is the Real Value of a Lost Customer?" *Journal of Service Research* 5 (3), 196–208.

Hui, Sam K., Jehoshua Eliashberg, and Edward I. George (2008), "DVD Preorder and Sales: An Optimal Stopping Approach." *Marketing Science* 27 (6), 1097–110.

Islam, Towhidul, Denzil G. Fiebig, and Nigel Meade (2002), "Modeling Multinational Telecommunications Demand with Limited Data." *International Journal of Forecasting* 18 (4), 605–624.

Islam, Towhidul, and Nigel Meade (1997), "The Diffusion of Successive Generations of a Technology: A More General Model." *Technological Forecasting and Social Change* 56 (1), 49–60.

Iyengar, Raghuram, Christophe Van den Bulte, and Thomas W. Valente (2008), "Opinion Leadership and Social Contagion in New Product Diffusion." Cambridge, Mass.: Marketing Science Institute, Report No. 08–120.

Jain, Dipak, Vijay Mahajan, and Eitan Muller (1991), "Innovation Diffusion in the Presence of Supply Restrictions." *Marketing Science* 10 (1), 83–90.

Jain, Dipak, Vijay Mahajan, and Eitan Muller (1995), "An Approach for Determining Optimal Product Sampling for the Diffusion of a New Product." *Journal of Product Innovation Management* 12 (2), 124–35.

Jiang, Zhengrui, Frank M. Bass, and Portia Isaacson Bass (2006), "The Virtual Bass Model and the Left–Hand Truncation Bias in Diffusion of Innovation Studies." *International Journal of Research in Marketing* 23 (1), 93–106.

Jones, J. Morgan, and Christopher J. Ritz (1991), "Incorporating Distribution into New Product Diffusion Models." *International Journal of Research in Marketing* 8 (2), 91–112.

Kalish, Shlomo, Vijay Mahajan, and Eitan Muller (1995), "Waterfall and Sprinkler New-Product Strategies in Competitive Global Markets." *International Journal of Research in Marketing* 12 (2), 105–19.

Karine, Eeva-Mari, Lauri Frank, and Kalle Laine (2004), "The Effect of Price on the Diffusion of Cellular Subscriptions in Finland." *Journal of Product and Brand Management* 13 (2), 192–9.

Kauffman, Robert J., and Angsana A. Techatassanasoontorn (2005), "International Diffusion of Digital Mobile Technology: A Coupled-Hazard State-Based Approach." *Information Technology and Management* 6 (2–3), 253–92.

Keehan, Sean, Andrea Sisko, Christopher Truffer, Sheila Smith, Cathy Cowan, John Poisal, and M. Kent Clemens (2008), "Health Spending Projections Through 2017." *Health Affairs* 27 (2), 145–55.

Kim, Namwoon, Eileen Bridges, and Rajendra K. Srivastava (1999), "A Simultaneous Model for Innovative Product Category Sales Diffusion and Competitive Dynamics." *International Journal of Research in Marketing* 16 (2), 95–111.

Kim, Namwoon, D. R. Chang, and Alan D. Shocker (2000), "Modeling Intercategory and Generational Dynamics for a Growing Information Technology Industry." *Management Science* 46 (4), 496–512.

Kim, Namwoon, Vijay Mahajan, and Rajendra K. Srivastava (1995), "Determining the Going Market Value of a Business in an Emerging Information Technology Industry: The Case of the Cellular Communications Industry." *Technological Forecasting and Social Change* 49 (3), 257–49.

Kohli, Rajeev, Donald R. Lehmann, and Jae Pae (1999), "Extent and Impact of Incubation Time in New Product Diffusion." *Journal of Product Innovation Management* 16 (2), 134–44.

Kossinets, Gueorgi, and Duncan J. Watts (2006), "Empirical Analysis of an Evolving Social Network." *Science* 311 (5757), 88–90.

Krider, Robert E., and Charles B. Weinberg (1998), "Competitive Dynamics and the Introduction of New Products: The Motion Picture Timing Game." *Journal of Marketing Research* 35 (1), 1–15.

Krishnan, Trichy V., Frank M. Bass, and Dipak C. Jain (1999), "Optimal Pricing Strategy for New Products." *Management Science* 45 (12), 1650–63.

Krishnan, Trichy V., Frank M. Bass, and V. Kumar (2000), "The Impact of Late Entrant on the Diffusion of a New Product/Service." *Journal of Marketing Research* 37 (2), 269–78.

Krishnan, Trichy V., and Dipak C. Jain (2006), "Optimal Dynamic Advertising Policy for New Products." *Management Science* 52 (12), 1957–69.

Krishnan, Trichy V., P.B. Seetharaman, and Demetrios Vakratsas (2007), "Size versus Slice of the Pie: Modeling Category and Brand Level SUV Sales." Singapore: National University of Singapore, Working Paper.

Kumar, Sunil, and Jayasgankar M. Swaminathan (2003), "Diffusion of Innovations under Supply Constraints." *Operations Research* 51 (6), 866–79

Kumar, V., Anish Nagpal, and Rajkumar Venkatesan (2002), "Forecasting Category Sales and Market Share for Wireless Telephone Subscribers: A Combined Approach." *International Journal of Forecasting* 18 (4), 583–603.

Kumar, V., and Trichy V. Krishnan (2002), "Research Note: Multinational Diffusion Models: An Alternative Framework." *Marketing Science* 21 (3), 318–32.

Landsman, Vardit, and Moshe Givon (2009), "The Diffusion of a New Service Combining Service Consideration and Brand Choice." *Quantitative Marketing and Economics*, forthcoming

Lattin, James, and John H. Roberts (1988), "The Role of Individual-Level Risk-Adjusted Utility in the Diffusion of Innovation." Palo Alto, Calif.: Stanford University, Working Paper.

Lee, Jonathan A., Peter Boatwright, and Wagner A. Kamakura (2003), "A Bayesian Model for Prelaunch Sales Forecasting of Recorded Music." *Management Science* 49 (2), 179–96.

Lehmann, Donald R., and Mercedes Esteban-Bravo (2006), "When Giving Some Away Makes Sense to Jump-Start the Diffusion Process." *Marketing Letters* 17 (4), 243–54.

Lehmann, Donald R., and Charles B. Weinberg (2000), "Sale Through Sequential Distribution Channels: An Application to Movies and Videos." *Journal of Marketing* 64 (3), 18–33.

Libai, Barak, Eitan Muller, and Renana Peres (2005), "The Role of Seeding in Multi-Market Entry." *International Journal of Research in Marketing* 22 (4), 375–93.

Libai, Barak, Eitan Muller, and Renana Peres (2009a), "The Influence of Within-Brand and Cross-Brand Word of Mouth on the Growth of Competitive Markets." *Journal of Marketing* 73 (2), 19–34.

Libai, Barak, Eitan Muller, and Renana Peres (2009b), "The Diffusion of Services." *Journal of Marketing Research* 46 (2), 163–75.

Lilien, Gary. L., Arvind Rangaswamy, and Christophe Van den Bulte (2000), "Diffusion Models: Managerial Applications and Software." In *New-Product Diffusion Models*, eds. Vijay Mahajan, Eitan Muller, and Yoram Wind, Chapter 12, 295–311. New York, N.Y.: Kluwer Academic Publishers.

Mahajan, Vijay (2009), *Africa Rising*. Philadelphia, Penn.: Wharton School Publishing.

Mahajan, Vijay, and Kamini Banga (2006), *The 86% Solution: How to Succeed in the Biggest Marketing Opportunity of the Next 50 Years*. Philadelphia, Penn.: Wharton School Publishing.

Mahajan, Vijay, and Eitan Muller (1994), "Will the 1992 Unification of the European Community Accelerate Diffusion of New Ideas, Products, and Technologies?" *Technological Forecasting and Social Change* 45 (3), 221–35.

Mahajan, Vijay, and Eitan Muller (1996), "Timing, Diffusion, and Substitution of Successive Generations of Technological Innovations: The IBM Mainframe Case." *Technological Forecasting and Social Change* 51 (2), 109–32.

Mahajan, Vijay, and Eitan Muller (1998), "When Is It Worthwhile Targeting the Majority Instead of the Innovators in a New Product Launch?" *Journal of Marketing Research* 35 (4), 488–95.

Mahajan, Vijay, Eitan Muller, and Frank M. Bass (1990), "New Product Diffusion Models in Marketing: A Review and Directions for Research." *Journal of Marketing* 54 (1), 1–26.

Mahajan, Vijay, Eitan Muller, and Frank Bass (1995), "Diffusion of New Products: Empirical Generalizations and Managerial Uses." *Marketing Science* 14 (2), 79–88.

Mahajan, Vijay, Eitan Muller, and Rajendra Srivastava (1990), "Determination of Adopter Categories Using Innovation Diffusion Models." *Journal of Marketing Research* 27 (1), 37–50.

Mahajan, Vijay, Eitan Muller, and Yoram Wind (2000), *New-Product Diffusion Models.* New York, N.Y.: Kluwer Academic Publishers.

Mahajan, Vijay, Subash Sharma, and Robert D. Buzzell (1993), "Assessing the Impact of Competitive Entry on Market Expansion and Incumbent Sales." *Journal of Marketing* 57 (3), 39–52.

Meade, Nigel, and Towhidul Islam (1998), "Technological Forecasting—Model Selection, Model Stability and Combining Models." *Management Science* 44 (8), 1115–30.

Meade, Nigel, and Towhidul Islam (2006), "Modeling and Forecasting the Diffusion of Innovation—A 25 Year Review." *International Journal of Forecasting* 22 (3), 519–45.

Mesak, Hani I. (1996), "Incorporating Price, Advertising, and Distribution into Diffusion Models of Innovation: Some Theoretical and Empirical Results." *Computers and Operations Research* 23 (10), 1007–23.

Mesak, Hani I., and Ali F. Darrat (2002), "Optimal Pricing of New Subscriber Services under Interdependent Adoption Processes." *Journal of Service Research* 5 (3), 140–53.

Mesak, Hani I., and Ali F. Darrat (2003), "An Empirical Inquiry into New Subscriber Services under Interdependent Adoption Processes." *Journal of Service Research* 6 (2), 180–92.

Mishra, Sanjay, Dongwook Kim, and Dae Hoon Lee (1996), "Factors Affecting New Product Success: Cross-Country Comparisons." *Journal of Product Innovation Management* 13 (6), 530–50.

Moe, Wendy, and Peter Fader (2002), "Using Advanced Purchase Orders to Forecast New Product Sales." *Marketing Science* 21 (3), 347–64.

Moldovan, Sarit, Jacob Goldenberg, and Amitava Chattopadhyay (2006), "What Drives Word-of-Mouth? The Roles of Product Originality and Usefulness." Cambridge, Mass.: Marketing Science Institute, Report No. 06-111.

Moon, Youngme (2003), "Microsoft: Positioning the Tablet PC." Cambridge, Mass.: Harvard Business School Case 9-502-051.

Moore, Geoffrey A. (1991), *Crossing the Chasm*. New York, N.Y.: HarperBusiness.

Muller, Eitan, and Guy Yogev (2006), "When Does the Majority Become a Majority? Empirical Analysis of the Time at Which Main Market Adopters Purchase the Bulk of Our Sales." *Technological Forecasting and Social Change* 73 (9), 1107–20.

Nair, Harikesh, Pradeep Chintagunta, and Jean-Pierre Dubé (2004), "Empirical Analysis of Indirect Network Effects in the Market for Personal Digital Assistants." *Quantitative Marketing and Economics* 2 (1), 23–58.

Neelamegham, Ramya, and Pradeep Chintagunta (1999), "A Bayesian Model to Forecast New Product Performance in Domestic and International Markets." *Marketing Science* 18 (2), 115–36.

Norton, John A., and Frank M. Bass (1987), "A Diffusion Theory Model of Adoption and Substitution for Successive Generations of High-Technology Products." *Management Science* 33 (9), 1069–86.

Norton, John A., and Frank M. Bass (1992), "The Evolution of Technological Generations: The Law of Capture." *Sloan Management Review* 33 (2), 66–77.

Ofek, Elie (2005), "Forecasting the Adoption of New Products." Cambridge, Mass.: Harvard Business School Case 9-505-062.

Padmanabhan, V., and Frank M. Bass (1993), "Optimal Pricing of Successive Generations of Product Advances." *International Journal of Research in Marketing* 10 (2), 185–207.

Pae, Jae H., and Donald R. Lehmann (2003), "Multigeneration Innovation Diffusion: The Impact of Intergeneration Time." *Journal of the Academy of Marketing Science* 31 (1), 36–45.

Parker, Philip M. (1994), "Aggregate Diffusion Forecasting Models in Marketing: A Critical Review." *International Journal of Forecasting* 10 (2), 353–80.

Parker, Philip, and Hubert Gatignon (1994), "Specifying Competitive Effects in Diffusion Models: An Empirical Analysis." *International Journal of Research in Marketing* 11 (1), 17–39.

Peres, Renana, Eitan Muller, and Vijay Mahajan (2010), "Innovation Diffusion and New Product Growth Models: A Critical Review and Research Directions." *International Journal of Research in Marketing*, forthcoming.

Peterson, Robert A., and Vijay Mahajan (1978), "Multi-product Growth Models." In *Research in Marketing*, ed. J. N. Sheth, 201–31. Greenwich, Conn.: JAI Press.

Prasad, Ashutosh, Bart Bronnenberg, and Vijay Mahajan (2004), "Product Entry Timing in Dual Distribution Channels: The Case of the Movie Industry." *Review of Marketing Science* [online] 2 (4).

Prasad, Ashutosh, and Vijay Mahajan (2003), "How Many Pirates Should a Software Firm Tolerate? An Analysis of Piracy Protection on the Diffusion of Software." *International Journal of Research in Marketing* 20 (4), 337–53.

Prins, Remco, and Peter C. Verhoef (2007), "Marketing Communication Drivers of Adoption Timing of a New E-Service among Existing Customers." *Journal of Marketing* 54 (5), 998–1014.

Putsis, William P., Sridhar Balasubramanian, Edward H. Kaplan, and Subrata K. Sen (1997), "Mixing Behavior in Cross-country Diffusion." *Marketing Science* 16 (4), 354–70.

Putsis, William P., and V. Srinivasan (2000), "Estimation Techniques for Macro Diffusion Models." In *New-Product Diffusion Models*, eds. Vijay Mahajan, Eitan Muller, and Yoram Wind, 263–91. New York, N.Y.: Kluwer Academic Publishers.

Radas, Sonja, and Steven M. Shugan (1998), "Seasonal Marketing and Timing New Product Introductions." *Journal of Marketing Research* 35 (3), 296–315.

Rahmandad, Hazhir, and John Streman (2008), "Heterogeneity and Network Structure in the Dynamics of Diffusion: Comparing Agent-Based and Differential Equation Models." *Management Science* 54 (5), 998–1014.

Reichheld, Frederick F. (1996), *The Loyalty Effect*. Cambridge, Mass.: Harvard Business School Press.

Reichheld, Frederick F. (2003), "The One Number You Need to Grow." *Harvard Business Review* 81 (12), 46–54.

Rindfleisch, Aric, and Christine Moorman (2001), "The Acquisition and Utilization of Information in New Product Alliances: A Strength-of-Ties Perspective." *Journal of Marketing* 65 (2), 1–18.

Roberts, John H., and James M. Lattin (2000), "Disaggregate-level Diffusion Models." In *New-Product Diffusion Models*, eds. Vijay Mahajan, Eitan Muller, and Yoram Wind, 207–36. New York, N.Y.: Kluwer Academic Publishers.

Robinson, Bruce, and Chet Lakhani (1975), "Dynamic Price Model for New-Product Planning." *Management Science* 21 (10), 1113–22.

Rogers, Everett M. (1995), *Diffusion of Innovations*. New York, N.Y.: Free Press.

Rohlfs, Jeffrey (2001), *Bandwagon Effects in High-Technology Industries*. Cambridge, Mass.: MIT Press.

Rosen, Emanuel (2000), *The Anatomy of Buzz*. New York, N.Y.: Doubleday.

Russell, Thomas (1980), "Comments on the Relationship Between Diffusion Rates, Experience Curves, and Demand Elasticities for Consumer Durable Technological Innovations." *Journal of Business* 53 (3), 69–73.

Savin, Sergei, and Christian Terwiesch (2005), "Optimal Product Launch Times in a Duopoly: Balancing Life-Cycle Revenues with Product Cost." *Operations Research* 53 (1), 26–47.

Sawhney, Mohanbir S., and Jehoshua Eliashberg (1996), "A Parsimonious Model for Forecasting Gross Box-Office Revenues of Motion Pictures." *Marketing Science* 15 (2), 113–31.

Schmittlein, David C., and Vijay Mahajan (1982), "Maximum Likelihood Estimation for an Innovation Diffusion Model of New Product Acceptance." *Marketing Science* 1 (10), 57–78.

Shaikh, Nazrul I., Arvind Rangaswamy, and Anant Balakrishnan (2006), "Modeling the Diffusion of Innovations Using Small-World Networks." University Park, Penn.: Penn State University, Working Paper.

Simmel, Georg (1957), "Fashion." *The American Journal of Sociology* 62 (6), 541–58.

Song, Inseong, and Pradeep K. Chintagunta (2003), "A Micromodel of New Product Adoption with Heterogeneous and Forward-Looking Consumers." *Quantitative Marketing and Economics* 1 (4), 371–407.

Srinivasan, Raji, Gary L. Lilien, and Arvind Rangaswamy (2004), "First in, First out? The Surprising Effects of Network Externalities on Pioneer Survival." *Journal of Marketing* 68 (1), 41–58.

Srinivasan, V., and Charlotte H. Mason (1986), "Non-linear Least Squares Estimation on New Product Diffusion Models." *Marketing Science* 5 (2), 169–78.

Stephen, Andrew T., and Jonah Berger (2009), "Creating Contagious: How Social Networks and Item Characteristics Combine to Spur Ongoing Consumption and Reinforce Social Epidemics." New York, N.Y.: Columbia University, Working Paper.

Stremersch, Stefan (2009), "Health and Marketing: The Emergence of a New Field of Research." *International Journal of Research in Marketing* 25 (4), 229–33.

Stremersch, Stefan, and Aurelie Lemmens (2009), "Sales Growth of New Pharmaceuticals across the Globe: The Role of Regulatory Regimes." *Marketing Science* 28 (4), 690–708.

Stremersch, Stefan, Eitan Muller, and Renana Peres (2009), "Does Growth Accelerate across Technology Generations?" *Marketing Letters*, forthcoming.

Stremersch, Stefan, and Gerard J. Tellis (2004), "Understanding and Managing International Growth of New Products." *International Journal of Research in Marketing* 21 (4), 421–38.

Stremersch, Stefan, Gerard J. Tellis, Philip H. Franses, and Jeroen L.G. Binken (2007), "Indirect Network Effects in New Product Growth." *Journal of Marketing* 71 (3), 52–74.

Sultan, Fareena, John. H. Farley, and Donald R. Lehmann (1990), "A Meta-analysis of Applications of Diffusion Models." *Journal of Marketing Research* 27 (1), 70–7.

Swami, Sanjeev, Jehoshua Eliashberg, and Charles B. Weinberg (1999), "Silverscreener: A Modeling Approach to Movie Screen Management." *Marketing Science* 18 (3), 352–72.

Takada, Hirokazu, and Dipak Jain (1991), "Cross-national Analysis of Diffusion of Consumer Durable Goods in Pacific Rim Countries." *Journal of Marketing* 55 (2), 48–54.

Talukdar, Debabrata, K. Sudhir, and Andrew Ainslie (2002), "Investigating New Product Diffusion across Products and Countries." *Marketing Science* 21 (1), 97–116.

Tellefsen, Thomas, and Hirokazu Takada (1999), "The Relationship Between Mass Media Availability and the Multicountry Diffusion of Consumer Products." *Journal of International Marketing* 7 (1), 77–96.

Tellis, Gerard J., Stefan Stremersch, and Eden Yin (2003), "The International Takeoff of New Products: The Role of Economics, Culture, and Country Innovativeness." *Marketing Science* 22 (2), 188–208.

Tellis, Gerard J., Eden Yin, and Rakesh Niraj (2009), "Does Quality Win? Network Effects Versus Quality in High-Tech Markets." *Journal of Marketing Research* 46 (2), 135–49.

The World Bank Report (2008), "Global Economic Prospects: Technology Diffusion in the Developing World."

Thompson, Scott A., and Rajiv K. Sinha (2008), "Brand Communities and New Product Adoption: The Influence and Limits of Oppositional Loyalty." *Journal of Marketing* 72 (6), 65–80.

Tucker, Catherine (2008), "Identitfying Formal and Informal Influence in Technology Adoption with Network Externalalities." *Management Science* 55 (12), 2024–39.

Vakratsas, Demetrios, and Ceren Kolsarici (2008), "A Dual-Market Diffusion Model for a New Prescription Pharmaceutical." *International Journal of Research in Marketing* 25 (4), 282–93.

van den Broek, Jan, and Hans Heesterbeek (2007), "Nonhomogeneous Birth and Death Models for Epidemic Outbreak Data." *Biostatistics* 8 (2), 453–67.

Van den Bulte, Christophe (2000), "New Product Diffusion Acceleration: Measurement and Analysis." *Marketing Science* 19 (4), 366–80.

Van den Bulte, Christophe (2002), "Want to Know How Diffusion Speed Varies across Countries and Products? Try Using a Bass Model." *PDMA Visions* 26 (4), 12–5.

Van den Bulte, Christophe (2004), "Multigeneration Innovation Diffusion and Intergeneration Time: A Cautionary Note." *Journal of the Academy of Marketing Science* 32 (3), 357–60.

Van den Bulte, Christophe, and Yogesh V. Joshi (2007), "New Product Diffusion with Influentials and Imitators." *Marketing Science* 26 (3), 400–21.

Van den Bulte, Christophe, and Gary L. Lilien (1997), "Bias and Systematic Change in the Parameter Estimates of Macro-Level Diffusion Models." *Marketing Science* 16 (4), 338–53.

Van den Bulte, Christophe, and Gary L. Lilien (2001), "Medical Innovation Revisited: Social Contagion Versus Marketing Effort." *American Journal of Sociology* 106 (5), 1409–35.

Van den Bulte, Christophe, and Stefan Stremersch (2004), "Social Contagion and Income Heterogeneity in New Product Diffusion: A Meta-Analytic Test." *Marketing Science* 23 (4), 530–44.

Van den Bulte, Christophe, and Stefan Stremersch (2008), "Contrasting Early and Late New Product Diffusion: Speed across Time, Products and Countries." Philadelphia Penn.: University of Pennsylvania, Wharton School of Business, Working Paper.

Van den Bulte, Christophe, and Stefan Wuyts (2007), *Social Networks and Marketing*. Cambridge, Mass.: Marketing Science Institute.

Van Everdingen, Yvonne M., Wouter B. Aghina, and Dennis Fok (2005), "Forecasting Cross-Population Innovation Diffusion: A Bayesian Approach." *International Journal of Research in Marketing* 22 (3), 293–308.

Van Everdingen, Yvonne M., Dennis Fok, and Stefan Stremersch (2009), "Modeling Global Spillover in New Product Takeoff." *Journal of Marketing Research* 46 (5), 637–52.

Venkatesan, Rajkumar, and V. Kumar (2002), "A Genetic Algorithms Approach to Growth Phase Forecasting of Wireless Subscribers." *International Journal of Forecasting* 18 (4), 625–46.

Wareham, Jonathan, Armando Levy, and Wei Shi (2004), "Wireless Diffusion and Mobile Computing: Implications for the Digital Divide." *Telecommunications Policy* 28 (5–6), 439–57.

Watts, Duncan, and Peter S. Dodds (2007), "Influentials, Networks, and Public Opinion Formation." *Journal of Consumer Research* 34 (4), 441–58.

WCIS database, World Cellular Information Service http://www.wcisdata.com/.

Weerahandi, Samaradasa, and S.R. Dalal (1992), "A Choice-Based Approach to the Diffusion of a Service: Forecasting Fax Penetration by Market Segments." *Marketing Science* 11 (1), 39–53.

Weimann, Gabriel (1994), *The Influentials: People Who Influence People.* Albany, N.Y.: State University of New York Press (SUNY).

Wuyts, Stefan, Stefan Stremersch, Christophe Van den Bulte, and Philip Hans Franses (2004), "Vertical Marketing Systems for Complex Products: A Triadic Perspective." *Journal of Marketing Research* 41 (4), 479–87.

Yeon, Seung-jun, Sang-hyun Park, and Sang-wook Kim (2006), "A Dynamic Diffusion Model for Managing Customer Expectations and Satisfaction." *Technological Forecasting and Social Change* 73 (6), 648–65.

Zeithaml, Valarie A., and Mary Jo Bitner (2003), *Services Marketing*, 3rd ed. New York, N.Y.: McGraw Hill.

Zufryden, Fred S. (1996), "Linking Advertising to Box Office Performance of New Film Releases: A Marketing Planning Model." *Journal of Advertising Research* 36 (4), 29–41.

Zufryden, Fred S. (2000), "Relating Web Site Promotion to the Box Office Performance of New Film Releases." *Journal of Advertising Research* 40 (1–2), 55–64.

About the Authors

Eitan Muller is Professor of Marketing at the Stern School of Business, New York University, and the Nathan Galston Professor of Hi-Tech Marketing at the Recanati Graduate School of Business Administration, Tel Aviv University. He earned a B.Sc. (with distinction) in mathematics from the Technion, Israel Institute of Technology, an MBA (with distinction) in marketing, and a Ph.D. in managerial economics from the Kellogg Graduate School of Management, Northwestern University. He was a visiting professor at several business schools at leading universities such as Northwestern University, University of Pennsylvania, the University of British Columbia, and the University of Texas at Austin. He has won several awards including the Harold H. Maynard Award for significant contribution to marketing theory and thought.

His work deals mainly with managerial issues of new product introduction, including answers to question such as: Will network externalities accelerate or decelerate the growth of a new product? How ubiquitous is the chasm phenomenon and what can firms do in order to cross it successfully? Under what conditions does it pay for an airline to increase ticket price over time as the flight date approaches rather than give last-minute deals? How can one measure the effects of word-of-mouth programs on a social network?

He has consulted major firms, mainly in the telecommunications industry via PricewaterhouseCoopers where he was a Subject Matter Expert.

Muller has published over 60 papers in journals in marketing and economics, such as the *Journal of Marketing, Journal of Marketing Research, Marketing Science, Management Science, American Economic Review, Rand Journal of Economics,* and *Journal of Economic Theory.* He is a member of the editorial review boards of the *Journal of Marketing* and the *Journal of Marketing Research,* and is an area editor of *Marketing Science* and the *International Journal of Research in Marketing.*

Renana Peres is Lecturer of Marketing in the Hebrew University of Jerusalem. She earned a B.Sc. (with distinction) in physics from the Hebrew University of Jerusalem, an MBA (with distinction) in marketing from Tel Aviv University, and a Ph.D. in marketing from the Recanati School of Business, Tel Aviv University. She has been spending the academic years 2008–2009 and 2009–2010 as a Visiting Professor in the marketing department at the Wharton School of Business.

Her work deals with modeling aggregate phenomena in complex systems, specifically in the context of new product growth. How do special types of consumer interactions influence the profitability of new products? What is the best way to seed marketing programs in the market? How do the characteristics of a social network influence the desired action of the firm? How do consumer-related metrics such as customer lifetime value and customer equity change in a growing market? Many of these questions are asked in a B2B context. For solving these questions, she applies complexity tools such as agent-based models, as well as standard diffusion tools research.

Peres is the founder of Persay Ltd., a subsidiary of Comverse Technology, which develops algorithms and tools for voice-based verification. She served as the company's first CEO.

She has published in the *Journal of Marketing Research*, *Journal of Marketing*, the *International Journal of Research in Marketing*, *Marketing Letters*, and the *Journal of Computational Neuroscience*. She is a member of the editorial review board of the *International Journal of Research in Marketing*, and was a board member of the ISCA SPLC interest group.

Vijay Mahajan holds the John P. Harbin Centennial Chair in Business at McCombs School of Business, University of Texas at Austin. He received a B.Tech in chemical engineering from the Indian Institute of Technology at Kanpur, an M.S. in chemical engineering and a Ph.D. in management from the University of Texas at Austin. He served as the Dean of the Indian School of Business in Hyderabad from 2002–2004.

Mahajan has published extensively in the areas of innovation diffusion, marketing research methods, and marketing strategy in such journals as the *Journal of Marketing Research*, *Journal of Marketing*, *Marketing Science*, and *Management Science*. He has also published ten books including his recent books, *The 86% Solution* and *Africa Rising*.

He has been invited by more than 100 universities and research institutions worldwide for research presentations. He edited the *Journal of Marketing Research*, and has consulted with Fortune 500 companies and delivered executive development programs worldwide.

About MSI

Founded in 1961, the Marketing Science Institute is a learning organization dedicated to bridging the gap between marketing science theory and business practice. MSI's worldwide network includes scholars from leading graduate schools of management and forward-looking managers from many of the world's most successful corporations.

As a nonprofit institution, MSI financially supports academic research for the development—and practical translation—of leading-edge marketing knowledge on topics of importance to business. Issues of key importance to business performance are identified by the Board of Trustees, which represents MSI corporations and the academic community. MSI supports studies by academics on these issues and disseminates the results through conferences and workshops, as well as through its publications series.

Related MSI Publications

Social Networks and Marketing by Christophe Van den Bulte and Stefan Wuyts
(Relevant Knowledge Series)

Report No.
09-210 "Diffusion Forecasts Using Social Interactions Data" by Olivier Toubia,
Jacob Goldenberg, and Rosanna Garcia
08-200 "Functional Data Analysis: A New Approach for Predicting Market
Penetration of New Products" by Ashish Sood, Gareth M. James, and
Gerard J. Tellis
08-121 "Modeling Global Spillover in New Product Takeoff" by Yvonne van
Everdingen, Stefan Stremersch, and Dennis Fok
08-120 "Opinion Leadership and Social Contagion in New Product Diffusion"
by Raghuram Iyengar, Christophe Van den Bulte, and Thomas Valente
08-105 "Online User Comments versus Professional Reviews: Differential
Influences on Pre-release Movie Evaluation" by Anindita Chakravarty,
Yong Liu, and Tridib Mazumdar
08-103 "A New Approach to Modeling the Adoption of New Products:
Aggregated Diffusion Models" by Olivier Toubia, Jacob Goldenberg,
and Rosanna Garcia
07-204 "Revisiting the Digital Divide: An Analysis of Mobile Technology Depth
and Service Breadth in the BRIC Countries" by Alina Chircu and Vijay
Mahajan
07-122 "The Determinants and Outcomes of Internet Banking Adoption" by
Lorin Hitt, Mei Xue, and Pei-yu Chen
07-121 "Global Takeoff of New Products: Culture's Consequences, Wealth of
Nations, or Vanishing Differences?" by Deepa Chandrasekaran and
Gerard J. Tellis
07-114 "Prerelease Forecasting via Functional Shape Analysis of the Online
Virtual Stock Market" by Natasha Foutz and Wolfgang Jank
07-111 "Growth Acceleration across Technology Generations" by Stefan
Stremersch and Eitan Muller

07-109 "The Effects of Attrition on the Growth and Equity of Competitive Services" by Barak Libai, Eitan Muller, and Renana Peres

06-124 "The Role of Expert versus Social Opinion Leaders in New Product Adoption" by Jacob Goldenberg, Donald R. Lehmann, Daniella Shidlovski, and Michal Master Barak

06-111 "What Drives Word-of-Mouth? The Roles of Product Originality and Usefulness" by Sarit Moldovan, Jacob Goldenberg, and Amitava Chattopadhyay

05-200f "Research on Innovation: A Review and Agenda for Marketing Science" by John Hauser, Gerard J. Tellis, and Abbie Griffin

05-118 "Can a Late Mover Use International Market Entry Strategy to Challenge the Pioneer?" by Marc Fischer, Venkatesh Shankar, and Michel Clement

04-108 "What Drives New Product Success? An Investigation across Products and Countries" by Katrijn Gielens and Jan-Benedict E. M. Steenkamp

03-120 "Cascades, Diffusion, and Turning Points in the Product Life Cycle" by Peter N. Golder and Gerard J. Tellis

02-121 "The International Takeoff of New Products: The Role of Economics, Culture, and Country Innovativeness" by Gerard J. Tellis, Stefan Stremersch, and Eden Yin

02-111 "The Market Evolution and Sales Take-off of Product Innovations" by Rajshree Agarwal and Barry L. Bayus

02-108 "What Is the True Value of a Lost Customer?" by John E. Hogan, Katherine N. Lemon, and Barak Libai

02-106 "From Density to Destiny: Using Spatial Analysis for Early Prediction of New Product Success" by Tal Garber, Jacob Goldenberg, Barak Libai, and Eitan Muller